THE CURIOUS CASE
of
LADY PURBECK

A SCANDAL OF THE XVIITH CENTURY

by

THOMAS LONGUEVILLE

The Author of

"The Life of Sir Kenelm Digby,"
"The Adventures of King James II.,"
"Marshal Turenne"
"The Life of a Prig," Etc.

First published in 1909

This edition published by Read Books Ltd.
Copyright © 2018 Read Books Ltd.
This book is copyright and may not be
reproduced or copied in any way without
the express permission of the publisher in writing

British Library Cataloguing-in-Publication Data
A catalogue record for this book is available
from the British Library

CONTENTS

PREFACE

THE curious case of Lady Purbeck is here presented without embellishment, much as it has been found in old books and old manuscripts, chiefly at the Record Office and at the British Museum. Readers must not expect to find any "well-drawn characters," "fine descriptions," "local colour," or "dramatic talent," in these pages, on each of which Mr. Dry-as-dust will be encountered. Possibly some writer of fiction, endowed with able hands directed by an imaginative mind, may some day produce a readable romance from the rough-hewn matter which they contain: but, as their author's object has been to tell the story simply, as it has come down to us, and, as much as was possible, to let the contemporaries of the heroine tell it in their own words, he has endeavoured to suppress his own imagination, his own emotions, and his own opinions, in writing it. He has the pleasure of acknowledging much useful assistance and kind encouragement in this little work from Mr. Walter Herries Pollock.

CHAPTER I.

"After this alliance,
Let tigers match with hinds, and wolves with sheep,
And every creature couple with its foe."

DRYDEN.

THE political air of England was highly charged with electricity. Queen Elizabeth, after quarrelling with her lover, the Earl of Essex, had boxed his ears severely and told him to "go to the devil;" whereupon he had left the room in a rage, loudly exclaiming that he would not have brooked such an insult from her father, and that much less would he tolerate it from a king in petticoats.

This well-known incident is only mentioned to give an idea of the period of English history at which the following story makes its start. It is not, however, with public, but with private life that we are to be here concerned; nor is it in the Court of the Queen, but in the humbler home of her Attorney-General, that we must begin. In a humbler, it is true, yet not in a very humble home; for Mr. Attorney Coke had inherited a good estate from his father, had married an heiress, in Bridget Paston, who brought him the house and estate of Huntingfield Hall, in Suffolk, together with a large fortune in hard cash; and he had a practice at the Bar which had never previously been equalled. Coke was in great sorrow, for his wife had died on the 27th of June, 1598, and such was the pomp with which he determined to bury her, that her funeral did not take place until the 24th of July. In his memorandum-book he wrote on the day of her death: "Most beloved and most excellent wife, she well and happily lived, and, as a true handmaid of the Lord, fell asleep in the Lord and now reigns in Heaven." Bridget had made good use of her time, for, although she died at the age of thirty-three, she had, according to Burke, seven children; but, according to Lord Campbell, ten.

As Bridget was reigning in Heaven, Coke immediately began to look about for a substitute to fill the throne which she had left vacant upon earth. Youth, great personal beauty and considerable wealth, thought this broken-hearted widower at the age of forty-six, would be good enough for him, and the weeks since the true handmaid of the Lord had left him desolate were only just beginning to blend into months, when he fixed his mind upon a girl likely to fulfil his very moderate requirements. He, a widower, naturally sought a widow, and, happily, he found a newly made one. Youth she had, for she was only twenty; beauty she must have had in a remarkable degree, for she was afterwards one of the lovely girls selected to act with the Queen of James I. in Ben Jonson's *Masque of Beauty*; and wealth she had in the shape of immense estates.

Elizabeth, grand-daughter of the great Lord Burghley, and daughter of Burghley's eldest son Thomas Cecil, some years later Earl of Exeter, had been married to the nephew and heir of Lord Chancellor Hatton. Not very long after her marriage her husband had died, leaving her childless and possessed of the large property which he had inherited from his uncle. This young widow was a woman not only of high birth, great riches, and exceptional beauty, but also of remarkable wit, and, as if all this were not enough, she had, in addition, a violent temper and an obstinate will. This Coke found out in her conduct respecting a daughter who eventually became Lady Purbeck, the heroine of our little story.

Romance was not wanting in the Attorney-General's second wooing; for he had a rival, whom Lord Campbell in his *Lives of the Chief Justices*, describes as "then a briefless barrister, but with

8

brilliant prospects," a man of thirty-five, who happened to be Lady Elizabeth's cousin. His name was Francis Bacon, afterwards Lord Chancellor, Baron Verulam, Viscount St. Albans, and the author of the *Novum Organum* as well of a host of other works, including essays on almost every conceivable subject. In the opinion of certain people, he was also the author of the plays commonly attributed to one William Shakespeare. This rival was good-looking, had a charming manner, and was brilliant in conversation, while his range of subjects was almost unlimited, whereas, the wooer in whom we take such an affectionate interest, was wrinkled, dull, narrow-minded, unimaginative, selfish, over-bearing, arrogant, illiterate, ignorant in almost everything except jurisprudence, of which he was the greatest oracle then living, and uninterested in everything except law, his own personal ambition, and money-making.

Shortly before Coke had marked the young and lovely Lady Elizabeth Hatton for his own, Bacon had not only paid his court to her in person, but had also persuaded his great friend and patron, Lord Essex, to use his influence in inducing her to marry him. Essex did so to the very best of his ability, a kind service for which Bacon afterwards repaid him after he had fallen—we have seen that his star was already in its decadence—by making every effort, and successful effort, to get him convicted of treason, sentenced to death, and executed.

Which of these limbs of the law was the beautiful heiress to select? She showed no inclination to marry Francis Bacon, and she was backed up in this disinclination by her relatives, the Cecils. The head of that family, Lord Burghley, Queen Elizabeth's Lord High Treasurer, was particularly proud of his second son, Robert, whom he had succeeded in advancing by leaps and bounds until he had become Secretary of State; and Burghley and the rest of his family feared a dangerous rival to Robert in the brilliant Bacon, who had already attracted the notice, and was apparently about to receive the patronage, of the Court. If Bacon should marry the famous beauty and become possessed of her large fortune, there was no saying, thought the Cecils, but that he might attain to such an exalted position as to put their own precocious Robert in the shade.

Bridget had not been in her grave four months when the great Lord Burghley died. Coke attended his funeral, and a funeral being obviously a fitting occasion on which to talk about that still more dreary ceremony, a wedding, Coke took advantage of it to broach the question of a marriage between himself and Lady Elizabeth Hatton. He broached it both to her father, the new Lord Burghley, and to her uncle, the much more talented Robert. Whatever their astonishment may have been, each of these Cecils promised to offer no opposition to the match. They probably reflected that the Attorney-General was a man in a powerful position, and that, with his own great wealth combined with that of Lady Elizabeth Hatton, he might possibly prove of service to the Cecil family in the future.

How the match, proposed under such conditions, came about, history does not inform us, but, within six months of Bridget's funeral, her widower embalmed her memory by marrying Elizabeth Hatton, a girl fifteen years her junior.

If any writer possessed of imagination should choose to make a novel on the foundation of this simple story, he may describe to his readers how the cross-grained and unattractive Coke contrived to induce the fair Lady Elizabeth Hatton to accept him for a husband. The present writer cannot say how this miracle was worked, for the simple reason that he does not know. One incident in connection with the marriage, however, is a matter of history. Elizabeth was not sufficiently proud of her prospective bride-groom to desire to stand beside him at a wedding before a large, fashionable, and critical assemblage in a London church. If he would have her at all, she insisted that he must take her in the only way in which he could get her, namely, by a clandestine marriage, in a private house, with only two or three witnesses.

Now, if there was one thing more than another in which Mr. Attorney Coke lived and moved and had his being, it was the law, to all offenders against which he was an object of terror; and such a great lawyer must have been fully aware that, by making a clandestine marriage in a private house, he would render himself liable to the greater excommunication, whereby, in addition to the minor annoyance of being debarred from the sacraments, he might forfeit the whole of his property and be subjected to perpetual imprisonment. To make matters worse, Archbishop Whitgift had just issued a pastoral letter to all the bishops in the province of Canterbury, condemning marriages in private houses at unseasonable hours, and forbidding under the severest penalties any marriage, except in a cathedral or in a parish church, during the canonical hours, and after proclamation of banns on three Sundays or holidays, or else with the license of the ordinary.

Rather than lose his prize, Coke, the great lawyer, determined to defy the law, and to run all risks, risks which the bride seemed anxious to make as great as possible; for, at her earnest request, or rather dictation, the pair were married in a private house, without license or banns, and in the evening, less than five months after Coke had made the entry in his diary canonising Bridget. As the Archbishop had been his tutor, Coke may have expected him to overlook this little transgression. Instead of this, the pious Primate at once ordered a suit to be instituted in his Court against the bridegroom, the bride, the parson who had married them, and the bride's father, Lord Burghley, who had given her away. Lord Campbell says that "a libel was exhibited against them, concluding for the 'greater excommunication' as the appropriate punishment."

Mr. Attorney now saw that there was nothing to be done but to kiss the rod. Accordingly, he made a humble and a grovelling submission, on which the Archbishop gave a dispensation under his great seal, a dispensation which is registered in the archives of Lambeth Palace, absolving all concerned from the penalties they had incurred, and, as if to complete the joke, alleging, as an excuse, ignorance of the law on the part of the most learned lawyer in the kingdom.

The newly married pair had not a single taste in common. The wife loved balls, masques, hawking, and all sorts of gaiety; she delighted in admiration and loved to be surrounded by young gallants who had served in the wars under Sydney and Essex, and who could flatter her with apt quotations from the verses of Spenser and Surrey. The husband, on the contrary, detested everything in the form of fun and frolic, loved nothing but law and money, loathed extravagance and cared for no society, except that of middle-aged barristers and old judges. As might be expected, the union of this singularly ill-assorted couple was a most unhappy one. Indeed it was a case of—

> "at home 'tis steadfast hate,
> And one eternal tempest of debate."[1]

Within a year of their marriage, that is to say in 1599, Lady Elizabeth Hatton, as she still called herself, had a daughter. Here again Burke and Lord Campbell are at variance. Burke says that by this marriage Coke had two daughters, Elizabeth, who died unmarried, and Frances, our heroine; whereas Lord Campbell says that Frances was born within a year of their marriage and makes no mention of any Elizabeth. It is pretty clear, from subsequent events, that, if there was an Elizabeth, she must have died very young, and that Frances must have been born almost as soon as was possible after the birth of her elder sister.[2]

The beginning of our heroine may make the end of our chapter. In the next she will not be seen at all; but, as will duly appear, the events therein recorded had a great—it might almost be said a supreme—influence on her fortunes.

FOOTNOTES:

[1] Young's *Love of Fame.*

[2] Most of the matter in this chapter has been taken from *The Lives of the Chief Justices of England*, by John, Lord Campbell. In two volumes. London: John Murray, 1849, Vol. I., p. 239 *seq.*, Chap. VII.

CHAPTER II.

"Now hatred is by far the longest pleasure,
Men love in haste, but they detest at leisure."

Don Juan, xiii., 16.

RIVALS in love, rivals in law, rivals for place, Coke and Bacon, while nominally friends, were implacable enemies, but they sought their ends by different methods. When James I. had ascended the throne, Bacon began at once to seek his favour; but Coke took no trouble whatever for that purpose, and he was not even introduced to the royal presence until several weeks after the accession. Bacon, then a K.C., held no office during the first four years of the new reign; but his literary fame and his skilful advocacy at the Bar excited the jealousy of Coke. On one occasion, Coke grossly insulted him in the Court of Exchequer, whereupon Bacon said: "Mr. Attorney, I respect you but I fear you not; and the less you speak of your own greatness, the more I will think of it." Coke angrily replied: "I think scorn to stand upon terms of greatness towards you, who are less than little— less than the least."

Lord Campbell says that Sir Edward Coke's arrogance to the whole Bar, and to all who approached him, now became almost insufferable, and that "his demeanour was particularly offensive to his rival"—Bacon. As to prisoners, "his brutal conduct ... brought permanent disgrace upon himself and upon the English Bar." When Sir Walter Raleigh was being tried for his life, but had not yet been found guilty, Coke said to him: "Thou art the

14

most vile and execrable traitor that ever lived. I want words sufficient to express thy viprous treasons." When Sir Everard Digby confessed that he deserved the vilest death, but humbly begged for mercy and some moderation of justice, Coke told him that he ought "rather to admire the great moderation and mercy of the King, in that, for so exorbitant a crime, no new torture answerable thereto was devised to be inflicted upon him," and that, as to his wife and children, he ought to desire the fulfilment of the words of the Psalm: "Let his wife be a widow and his children vagabonds: let his posterity be destroyed, and in the next generation let his name be quite put out." According to Lord Campbell, Coke's "arrogance of demeanour to all mankind is unparalleled."

Towards the end of the reign of Elizabeth, Coke, as Attorney-General, had had another task well suited to his taste, that of examining the prisoners stretched on the rack, at the Tower. Volumes of examinations of prisoners under torture, in Coke's own handwriting, are still preserved at the State Paper Office, which, says Campbell, "sufficiently attest his zeal, assiduity and hard-heartedness in the service.... He scrupulously attended to see the proper degree of pain inflicted." Yet this severe prosecutor, bitter advocate and cruel examiner, became a Chief Justice of tolerable courtesy, moderate severity, and unimpeachable integrity.

If he had everything his own way in the criminal court and the torture chamber, Coke did not find his wishes altogether unopposed in his family. To begin with, he suffered the perpetual insult of the refusal on the part of his wife to be called by his name. If her first husband had been of higher rank, it might have been another matter: but both were only knights, and it was a parallel case to the widow Jones, after she had married Smith, insisting upon still calling herself Mrs. Jones. Lady Elizabeth defended her conduct on this point as follows:[3] "I returned this answer: that if Sir Edward Cooke would bury my first husband accordingto to his own directions, and also paie such small legacys as he gave to divers of his friends, in all cominge not to above £700 or £900, at the most that was left unperformed, he having all Sir William Hatton's goods & lands to a large proportion, then would I willingly stile myself by his name. But he never yielded, so I consented not to the other." Whether Hatton or Coke, as an Earl's daughter she was Lady Elizabeth, by which name alone let us know her.

Campbell states that, after the birth of Frances, Sir Edward and Lady Elizabeth "lived little together, although they had the prudence to appear to the world to be on decent terms till the heiress was marriageable." Coke had been astute enough to secure a comfortable country-house, at a very convenient distance from London, through Lady Elizabeth. Her ladyship had held a mortgage upon Stoke Pogis, a place that belonged formerly to the Earls of Huntingdon,[4] and Coke, either by foreclosing or by selling, obtained possession of the property. As it stood but three or four miles to the north of Windsor, the situation was excellent. [5] Sir Edward's London house was in the then fashionable quarter of Holborn, a place to which dwellers in the city used to go for change of air.[6] As Coke and his wife generally quarrelled when together, the husband was usually at Holborn[7] when the wife was at Stoke, and *vice-versâ*. It was almost impossible that Miss Frances should not notice the strained relations between her parents. Nothing could have been much worse for the education of their daughter than their constant squabblings; and, unless she differed greatly from most other daughters, she would take advantage of their mutual antipathies to play one against the other, a pleasing pastime, by means of which young ladies, blessed with quarrelsome parents, often obtain permissions and other good things of this world, which otherwise they would have to do without.

Lady Elizabeth found a friend and a sympathiser in her domestic worries. Francis Bacon, the former lover of her fortune, if not of her person, became her consoler and her counsellor. Let not the reader suppose that these pages are so early to be sullied by

16

a scandal. Nothing could have been farther from reproach than the marital fidelity of Lady Elizabeth, but it must have gratified Bacon to annoy the man who had crossed and conquered him in love, or in what masqueraded under that name, by fanning the flames of Lady Elizabeth's fiery hatred against her husband. Hitherto, Coke had had it all his own way. He had snubbed and insulted Bacon in the law courts, and he had snatched a wealthy and beautiful heiress from his grasp. The wheel of fortune was now about to take a turn in the opposite direction.

About the year 1611, King James entertained the idea of reigning as an absolute sovereign. Archbishop Bancroft flattered him in this notion, and suggested that the King ought to have the privilege of "judging whatever cause he pleased in his own person, free from all risk of prohibition or appeal." James summoned the judges to his Council and asked whether they consented to this proposal. Coke replied:—

"God has endowed your Majesty with excellent science as well as great gifts of nature; but your Majesty will allow me to say, with all reverence, that you are not learned in the laws of this your realm of England, and I crave leave to remind your Majesty that causes which concern the life or inheritance, or goods or fortunes of your subjects are not to be decided by natural reason, but by the artificial reason and judgment of law, which law is an art which requires long study and experience before that a man can attain to the cognizance of it."

On hearing this, James flew into a rage and said: "Then am I to be *under* the law—which it is treason to affirm?"

To which Coke replied: "Thus wrote Braxton: 'Rex non debet esse sub homine, sed sub *Deo et Lege.*'"[8]

Coke had the misfortune to offend the King in another matter. James issued proclamations whenever he thought that the existing law required amendment. A reply was drawn up by Coke, in which he said: "The King, by his proclamation or otherwise, cannot change any part of the common law, or statute law, or the customs of the realm." This still further aggravated

James.

Meanwhile Bacon, now Attorney-General, was high in the King's favour, and he was constantly manoeuvring in order to bring about the downfall of his rival. He persuaded James to remove Coke from the Common Pleas to the King's Bench—a promotion, it is true, but to a far less lucrative post. This greatly annoyed Coke, who, on meeting Bacon, said: "Mr. Attorney, this is all your doing." For a time Coke counteracted his fall in James's favour by giving £2,000 to a "Benevolence," which the King had asked for the pressing necessities of the Crown, a benevolence to which the other judges contributed only very small sums. This fair weather, however, was not to be of long duration.

In 1616 Coke again offended the King. Bacon had declared his opinion that the King could prohibit the hearing of any case in which his prerogative was concerned. In the course of a trial which shortly afterwards took place, Bacon wrote to the judges that it was "his Majesty's express pleasure that the farther argument of the said cause be put off till his Majesty's farther pleasure be known upon consulting him." In a reply, drawn up by Coke and signed by the other judges, the King was told that "we have advisedly considered of the said letter of Mr. Attorney, and with one consent do hold the same to be contrary to law, and such as we could not yield to by our oaths."

James was furious. He summoned the judges to Whitehall and gave them a tremendous scolding. They fell on their knees and all were submissive except Coke, who boldly said that "obedience to his Majesty's command ... would have been a delay of justice, contrary to law, and contrary to the oaths of the judges."

Although Coke was now in terrible disgrace at Court, he might have retained his office of Chief Justice, if he would have sanctioned a job for Villiers, the new royal favourite. George Villiers, a young man of twenty-four, since the fall of the Earl of Somerset had centralised all power and patronage in his own hands. The chief clerkship in the Court of King's Bench, a sinecure worth £4,000 a year, was falling vacant, and Villiers

wished to have the disposal of it. The office was in the gift of
Coke, and, when Bacon asked that its gift should be placed in the
hands of Villiers, Coke flatly refused and thus offended the most
powerful man in England. Nothing then became bad enough for
Coke and nothing in Coke could be good. His reports of cases
were carefully examined by Bacon, who pointed out to the King
many "novelties, errors, and offensive conceits" in them. The
upshot of the whole matter was that Coke was deprived of office.
When the news was communicated to him, says a contemporary
letter, "he received it with dejection and tears."[9]

It would be natural to suppose that by this time Bacon had
done enough to satisfy his vengeance upon Coke. But no! He
must needs worry him yet further by an exasperating letter, from
which some extracts shall be given. It opens with a good deal of
scriptural quotation as to the wholesomeness of affliction. Then
Bacon proceeds to say:[10] "Afflictions level the mole-hills of pride,
plough the heart and make it fit for Wisdom to sow her seed,
and for grace to bring forth her increase. Happy is that man,
therefore, both in regard of Heavenly and earthly wisdom, that
is thus wounded to be cured, thus broken to be made straight,
thus made acquainted with his own imperfections that he may
be perfect. Supposing this to be the time of your affliction, that
which I have propounded to myself is, by taking the seasonable
advantage, like a true friend (though far unworthy to be counted
so) to show your shape in a glass.... Yet of this resolve yourself,
it proceedeth from love and a true desire to do you good, that
you, knowing what the general opinion is may not altogether
neglect or contemn it, but mend what you may find amiss in
yourself.... First, therefore, behold your Errors: In discourse
you delight to speak too much.... Your affections are entangled
with a love of your own arguments, though they be the weaker....
Secondly, you cloy your auditory: when you would be observed,
speech must either be sweet, or short. Thirdly, you converse with
Books, not Men ... who are the best Books. For a man of action &
employment you seldom converse, & then but with underlings;

not freely but as a schoolmaster with his scholars, ever to teach, never to learn.... You should know many of these tales you tell to be but ordinary, & many other things, which you repeat, & serve in for novelties to be but stale.... Your too much love of the world is too much seen, when having the living" [income] "of £10,000, you relieve few or none: the hand that hath taken so much, can it give so little? Herein you show no bowels of compassion.... We desire you to amend this & let your poor Tenants in Norfolk find some comfort, where nothing of your Estate is spent towards their relief, but all brought up hither, to the impoverishing of your country.... When we will not mind ourselves, God (if we belong to him) takes us in hand, & because he seeth that we have unbridled stomachs, therefore he sends outward crosses." And Bacon ends by commending poor Coke "to God's Holy Spirit ... beseeching Him to send you a good issue out of all these troubles, & from henceforth to work a reformation in all that is amiss, & a resolute perseverance, proceeding, & growth, in all that is good, & that for His glory, the bettering of yourself, this Church & Commonwealth; whose faithful servant whilst you remain, I am a faithful servant unto you."

If ever there was a case of adding insult to injury, surely this piece of canting impertinence was one of the most outrageous.

FOOTNOTES:

[3] *Life of Sir Edward Coke.* By H.W. Woolrych. London: J. & W.T. Clarke, 1826, pp. 145-48.

[4] Lipscomb's *History and Antiquities of the Co. of Bucks*, 1847, Vol. IV., p. 548.

[5] Gray made the churchyard of Stoke Pogis the scene of his famous Elegy, and he was buried there in 1771.

[6] *Ency. Brit.*, Vol. XIV. Article on London.

[7] Lady Elizabeth's house in Holborn was called Hatton House. A letter (*S.P. Dom.*, James I., 13th July, 1622) says: "Lady Hatton

sells her house in Holborn to the Duke of Lennox, for £12,000." Another letter (ib. 26th February, 1628) says that "Lady Hatton complained so much of her bargain with the Duchess of Richmond for Hatton House, that the Duchess has taken her at her word and left it on her hands, whereby she loses £1,500 a year, and £6,000 fine."

[8] "Under no man's judgment should the King lie; but under God and the law only."

[9] Letter from John Castle. See D'Israeli's *Character of James I.*, p. 125.

[10] *Cabala Sive Scrina Sacra*: Mysteries of State and Government. In *Letters of Illustrious Persons, etc.* London: Thomas Sawbridge and others, 1791, p. 86.

CHAPTER III.

"Marriage is a matter of more worth
Than to be dealt in by attorneyship."

Henry VI., I., v., 5.

IF Bacon flattered himself that he had extinguished Coke for good and all, he was much mistaken. It must have alarmed him to find that Lady Elizabeth, after constant quarrels with her husband and ceasing to live with him, had taken his part, now that he had been dismissed from office, that she had solicited his cause at the very Council table,[11] and that she had quarrelled with both the King and the Queen about the treatment of her husband, with the result that she had been forbidden to go to Court, and had begun to live again with Coke, taking with her her daughter, now well on in her 'teens.

There was a period of hostilities, however, early in the year 1617. Sir Edward and Lady Elizabeth went to law about her jointure. In May Chamberlain wrote to Carleton:—

"The Lord Coke & his lady hath great wars at the council table. I was there on Wednesday, but by reason of the Lord Keeper's absence, there was nothing done. What passed yesterday I know not yet: but the first time she came accompanied with the Lord Burghley" (her eldest brother), "& his lady, the Lord Danvers" (her maternal grandfather), "the Lord Denny" (her brother-in-law), "Sir Thomas Howard" (her nephew, afterwards first Earl of Berkshire) "& his lady, with I know not how many more, & declaimed bitterly against him, and so carried herself that divers said Burbage" [the celebrated actor of that time] "could not have acted better. Indeed, it seems he [Sir Edward Coke] hath carried himself very simply, to say no more, in divers matters: and no doubt he shall be sifted thoroughly, for the King is much incensed against him, & by his own weakness he hath lost those few friends he had."

It is clear from this letter that, although her husband was one of the greatest lawyers of the day, Lady Elizabeth was not at all afraid of pitting herself against him in Court, where indeed she seems to have proved the better pleader of the pair.

This dispute was patched up. On 4th June Chamberlain wrote: "Sir Edward Coke & his Lady, after so much animosity and wrangling, are lately made friends; & his curst heart hath been forced to yield more than ever he meant; but upon this agreement he flatters himself that she will prove a very good wife." So Coke and his "very good wife" settled down together again. We shall see presently whether there was to be a perpetual peace between them.

While Bacon was meditating an information against Sir Edward Coke in the Star Chamber for malversation of office, in the hope that a heavy fine might be imposed upon him, Coke also was plotting. He discovered that Bacon, who had been made Lord Keeper early in the year 1617, had had his head turned by his promotion and had become giddy on his pinnacle of greatness; or, to use Bacon's own words, that he was suffering acutely from an "unbridled stomach." Of this Coke determined to take advantage.

Looking back upon his own fall, Coke considered that the final crash had been brought about not, as Bacon had insinuated in his letter, by offending the Almighty, but by offending Villiers, now Earl of Buckingham, and he came to the conclusion that his best hope of recovering his position would be to find some method of doing that Earl a service. Now, Buckingham had an elder brother, Sir John Villiers, who was very poor, and for whom he was anxious to pick up an heiress. The happy thought struck

Coke that, as all his wife's property was entailed on her daughter, Frances, he might secure Buckingham's support by selling the girl to Buckingham's brother, for the price of Buckingham's favour and assistance. It was most fortunate that Frances was exceedingly beautiful, and that Sir John Villiers was unattractive and much older than she was; because this would render the amount of patronage, due in payment by Buckingham to Coke, so much the greater.

James I. and Buckingham had gone to Scotland. In the absence of the King and the Court, Bacon, as Lord Keeper, was one of the greatest men left in London, and quite the greatest in his own estimation. Misled by this idea of his own importance, he was imprudent enough to treat his colleague, Winwood, the Secretary of State, with as little ceremony as if he had been a junior clerk, thereby incurring the resentment of that very high official. Common hatred of Bacon made a strong bond of union between Coke and Winwood, and Winwood joined readily in the plot newly laid by Coke.

Sir John Villiers was already acquainted with Coke's pretty daughter; and, when Coke went to him, suggested a match, and enlarged upon the fortune to which she was sole heiress, Sir John professed to be over head and ears in love with her, and observed that "although he would have been well pleased to have taken her in her smoke [smock], he should be glad, by way of curiosity, to know how much could be assured by marriage settlement upon her and her issue."[12] With some reluctance Sir Edward Coke then entered into particulars, and the match was regarded as settled by both sides.

Everything having been now satisfactorily arranged, it occurred to Coke that possibly the time had arrived for informing, first his wife, and afterwards his daughter, of the marriage to which he had agreed.

Sir Edward had often seen his wife in a passion, and he had frequently been a listener to torrents of abuse from her pretty lips and caustic tongue. Although he had been notorious as the rudest member of the Bar, he had generally come off second best in his frequent battles of words with his beautiful helpmate. Stolid and unimpressible as he was, he can hardly have been impervious to the effects of the verbal venom with which she had constantly stung him. But all this had been mere child's play in comparison with her fury on being informed that, without so much as consulting her, her husband had definitely settled a match for her only child with a portionless knight. A new weapon was lying ready to her hand, and she made every possible use of it. It consisted in the fact that, much as she and her husband had quarrelled and lived apart, she had returned to him in the hour of his tribulation, had fought his battles before the King and the Council, and had even braved the royal displeasure and endured exile from the Court, rather than desert him in his need. She bitterly reproached him for repaying her constancy and sacrifices on his behalf by selling her daughter without either inquiring as to the mother's wishes, or even informing that mother of his intention.

If Lady Elizabeth was infuriated at the news of the match, her daughter was frenzied. She detested Sir John Villiers, and she implored her parents never again to mention the question of her marrying him. The mother and daughter were on one side and the father on the other; neither would yield an inch, and Hatton House, Holborn, became the scene of violent invective and bitter weeping.

Buckingham is said to have promised Coke that, if he would bring about the proposed marriage, he should have his offices restored to him. Buckingham's mother, Lady Compton, also warmly supported the project. She was what would now be called "a very managing woman." Since the death of Buckingham's father, she had had two husbands, Sir William Rayner and Sir Thomas Compton,[13] brother to the Earl of Northampton. She was in high favour at Court, and she was created Countess of Buckingham just a year later than the time with which we are now dealing. As Buckingham favoured the match, of course the King favoured it also; and, as has been seen, Winwood, the Secretary of State, favoured it, simply because Bacon did not.

On the other side, among the active opponents of the match, were Bacon the Lord Keeper, Lord and Lady Burghley, Lord Danvers, Lord Denny, Sir Thomas and Lady Howard, and Sir Edmund and Lady Withipole.

Suddenly, to Coke's great satisfaction, Lady Elizabeth became, as he supposed, calm and quiet. It was his habit to go to bed at nine o'clock, and to get up very early. One night he went to bed at his usual hour, under the impression that his wife was settling down nicely and resigning herself to the inevitable. While he was in his beauty-sleep, soon after ten, that excellent lady quietly left the house with her daughter, and walked some little distance to a coach, which she had engaged to be in waiting for them at an appointed place. In this coach they travelled by unfrequented and circuitous roads, until they arrived at a house near Oatlands, a place belonging to the Earl of Argyll, but rented at that time by Lady Elizabeth's cousin, Sir Edmund Withipole. The distance from Holborn to Oatlands, as the crow flies, is about twenty miles; but, by the roundabout roads which the fugitives took in order to prevent attempts to trace them, the distance must have been considerable, and the journey, in the clumsy coach of the period, over the rutted highways and the still worse by-roads of those times, must have been long and wearisome. Oatlands is close to Weybridge, to the south-west of London, in Surrey, just over the boundary of Middlesex and about a mile to the south of the river Thames.

In Sir Edmund Withipole's house Lady Elizabeth and her daughter lived in the strictest seclusion, and all precautions were taken to prevent the place of their retreat from becoming known. And great caution was necessary, for Lady Elizabeth and Frances were almost within a dozen miles of Stoke Pogis, their country home; so that they would have been in danger of being recognised, if they had appeared outside the house.

But Lady Elizabeth was not idle in her voluntary imprisonment.

She conceived the idea that the best method of preventing a match which she disliked for her daughter would be to make one of which she could approve. Accordingly she offered Frances to young Henry de Vere, eighteenth Earl of Oxford. Although to a lesser extent, like Sir John Villiers, he was impecunious and on the look out for an heiress, his father—who was distinguished for having been one of the peers appointed to sit in judgment on Mary, Queen of Scots, for having had command of a fleet to oppose the Armada, for his success in tournaments, for his comedies, for his wit, and for introducing the use of scents into England—having dissipated the large inheritance of his family.

Undoubtedly, Lady Elizabeth was a woman of considerable resource; but, with all her virtues, she was not over-scrupulous; for, as Lord Campbell says,[14] to induce her daughter to believe that Oxford was in love with her, she "showed her a forged letter, purporting to come from that nobleman, which asseverated that he was deeply attached to her, and that he aspired to her hand." Lady Elizabeth was apparently of opinion that everything—and everything includes lying and forgery—is fair in love and war.

FOOTNOTES:

[11] Chamberlain, in a letter dated 22nd June, 1616.

[12] A quotation given by Lord Campbell (Vol. I., p. 297); but he does not state his authority.

[13] Arthur Wilson, in his life of James I. (*Camden, History of England*, Vol. II., p. 727), tells the following story about Sir T. Compton whom he calls "a low spirited man." "One Bird, a roaring Captain, was the more insolent against him because he found him slow & backward." After many provocations, Bird "wrought so upon his cold temper, that Compton sent him a challenge." On receiving it, Bird told Compton's second that he would only accept the challenge on condition that the duel should take place in a saw-pit, "Where he might be

sure Compton could not run away from him." When both combatants were in the saw-pit, Bird said: "Now, Compton, thou shalt not escape me," and brandished his sword above his head. While he was doing this, Compton "in a moment run him through the Body; so that his Pride fell to the ground, and there did sprawl out its last vanity."

CHAPTER IV.

"There is no such thing as perfect secrecy."

—South's Sermons.

As might be expected, the whereabouts of the place for concealment of Lady Elizabeth and her daughter leaked out and reached the ears of Sir Edward Coke, who immediately applied to the Privy Council for a warrant to search for his daughter. Bacon opposed it. Indeed, it is said that Bacon had not only been all the time aware of the place of the girl's retreat, but had also joined actively in the plot to convey her to it. Because it was difficult to obtain a search-warrant from the Privy Council, Coke got an order to the same effect from Winwood, the Secretary of State;[15] and, although this order was of doubtful regularity, Coke determined to act upon it.

In July, 1617, Coke mustered a band of armed men, made up of his sons (Bridget's sons), his servants and his dependents. He put on a breastplate, and, with a sword at his side and pistols in the holsters of his saddle, he placed himself at the head of his little army, and gallantly led it to Oatlands to wage war upon his wife.

On arriving at the house which he went to besiege, he found no symptoms of any garrison for its defence. All was quiet, as if the place were uninhabited, the only sign that an attack was expected being that the gate leading to the house was strongly bolted and barred. To force the gate open, if a work requiring hard labour, was one of time, rather than of difficulty: and, when it had been accomplished, the general courageously led his troops from the outer defences to the very walls of the enemy's—that is to say of his wife's—castle.

The door of the house was found to be a very different thing from the gate. The besiegers knocked, and pounded, and thumped, and pushed, and battered: but that door withstood all their efforts. Again and again Coke, with a loud voice, demanded his child, in the King's name. "Remember," roared he to those within, "if we should kill any of your people, it would be justifiable homicide; but, if any of you should kill one of us, it would be MURDER!"[16]

To this opinion of the highest legal authority, given gratis, silence gave consent; for no reply was returned from the fortress, in which the stillness must have made the attackers afraid that the foes had fled. And then the bang, bang, banging on the door began afresh.

One of Coke's lieutenants suddenly bethought him of a flank attack, and, after sneaking round the house, this warrior adopted the burglar's manoeuvre of forcing open a window, on the ground floor. One by one the valiant members of Coke's little army climbed into the house by this means, and the august person of the ex-Lord Chief Justice himself was squeezed through the aperture. Nobody appeared to oppose their search; but preparations to prevent it had evidently been made with great care; for Chamberlain wrote that they had to "brake open divers doors."

Room after room was searched in vain; but, at last, Lady Elizabeth and Frances were discovered hidden in a small closet. Both the father and the mother clasped their daughter in their arms almost at the same moment. The daughter clung to the mother; the father clung to the daughter. Sir Edward pulled; Lady Elizabeth pulled; and, after a violent struggle between the husband and the wife, Coke succeeded in wrenching the weeping girl from her mother's arms.[17] Without a moment's parley with his defeated antagonist, he dragged away his prey, took her out of the house, placed her on horseback behind one of her half-brothers, and started off with his whole cavalcade for his house at Stoke Pogis.

The writer is old enough to have seen farmers' wives riding behind their husbands, on pillions. Most uncomfortable sitting those pillions appeared to afford, and he distinctly remembers the rolling movements to which the sitters seemed to be subjected. This was when the pace was at a walk or a slow jog. But the unfortunate Frances must have been rolled and bumped at speed; for there was a pursuit. In his already quoted letter to Carleton, Chamberlain says that Sir Edward Coke's "lady was at his heels, and, if her coach had not held"—*i.e.*, stuck in the mud of the appalling roads of the period—"in the pursuit after him, there was like to be strange tragedies." Miss Coke must have been long in forgetting that enforced ride of at least a dozen long miles, on a pillion behind a brother, and as a prisoner surrounded by an armed force.

Campbell states that, on reaching Stoke Pogis, Coke locked his daughter "in an upper chamber, of which he himself kept the key." Possibly, Sir John Villiers' mother, Lady Compton, may have been there, in readiness to receive her; for Chamberlain says that Coke "delivered his daughter to the Lady Compton, Sir John's mother; but, the next day, Edmondes, Clerk of the Council, was sent with a warrant to have the custody of the lady at his own house." This was probably Bacon's doing.

Among the manuscripts at Trinity College, Cambridge, is a letter[18] written from the Inner Temple to Mrs. Ann Sadler, a daughter of Sir Edward Coke by his first wife. From this we learn that, on finding herself robbed of her daughter, Lady Elizabeth hastened to London to seek the assistance of her friend Bacon. In driving thither her coach was "overturned." We saw that it had "held" in the heavy roads when she was chasing her husband in it, and very likely its wheels may have become loosened in some ruts on that occasion. An upset in a carriage, however, was a common occurrence in those days, and, nothing daunted, Lady Elizabeth managed to complete her journey to the house of

Bacon in London.

When she reached it, she was told that the Lord Keeper was unwell and in his room, asleep. She persuaded "the door-keeper" to take her to the sitting-room next to his bedroom, in order that she might be "the first to speak with him after he was stirring." The "door-keeper fulfilled her desire and in the meantime gave her a chair to rest herself in." Then he most imprudently left her, and she had not been alone long when "she rose up and bounced against my Lord Keeper's door." The noise not only woke up the sleeping Bacon, but "affrighted him" to such an extent that he called for help at the top of his voice. His servants immediately came rushing to his room. Doubtless he was relieved at seeing them; but his feelings may have been somewhat mixed when Lady Elizabeth "thrust in with them." He was on very friendly terms with her; but it was disconcerting to receive a lady from his bed when he was half awake and wholly frightened, especially when, as the correspondent describes it, the condition of that lady was like that of "a cow that had lost her calf."

The upshot of this rather unusual visit was that Lady Elizabeth got Bacon's warrant, as Lord Keeper, and also that of the Lord Treasurer "and others of the Council, to fetch her daughter from the father and bring them both to the Council."

At that particular time Bacon had just made a blunder. He was well aware of Buckingham's high favour with the King; but he scarcely realised its measure. Indeed, since he had seen him last, and during the time that the King had been in Scotland, Buckingham's influence over James had increased enormously. It is true that Bacon had enlisted the services of Buckingham to defeat Coke, and that he had used him as a tool to secure the office of Lord Keeper: but, as the occupier of that exalted position, he considered himself secure enough to take his own line, and even to offer Buckingham some fatherly advice, as will presently appear.

Bacon now made another attack upon his enemy by summoning Coke before the Star Chamber on a charge of breaking into a private house with violence. On receiving this summons, Coke wrote to Buckingham, who was with the King in the North, complaining that his wife, the Withipoles, and their confederates, had conveyed his "dearest daughter" from his house, "in most secret manner, to a house near Oatland, which Sir Edmund Withipole had taken for the summer of my Lord Argyle." Then he said: "I, by God's wonderful providence finding where she was, together with my sons and ordinary attendants did break open two doors, & recovered my daughter." His object, he said was, "First & principally, lest his Majesty should think I was of confederacy with my wife in conveying her away, or charge me with want of government in my household in suffering her to be carried away, after I had engaged myself to his Majesty for the furtherance of this match."

Buckingham, at about the same time that he received Coke's letter, received one in a very different tone from Bacon, in which he said:[19] "Secretary Winwood has busied himself with a match between Sir John Villiers & Sir Edward Coke's daughter, rather to make a faction than out of any good affection to your lordship. The lady's consent is not gained, *nor her mother's, from whom she expecteth a great fortune.* This match, out of my faith & freedom to your lordship, I hold very inconvenient, both for your mother, brother, & yourself."

"First. He shall marry into a disgraced house, which in reason of state, is never held good."

"Next. He shall marry into a troubled house of man & wife, which in religion and Christian discretion is not liked."

"Thirdly. Your lordship will go near to lose all such of your friends as are adverse to Sir Edward Coke (myself only except, who, out of a pure love & thankfulness, shall ever be firm to you).... Therefore, my advice is, & your lordship shall do yourself a great honour, if, according to religion & the law of God, your lordship will signify unto my lady, your mother, that your desire is that the marriage be not pressed or proceeded in without the consent of both parents, & so either break it altogether, or defer any further delay in it (sic) till your lordship's return."

A few days later, on the 25th of July, Bacon wrote to an even greater man than Buckingham, namely, to the King himself. "If," said he, "there be any merit in drawing on this match, your Majesty should bestow thanks, not upon the zeal of Sir Edward Coke to your Majesty, nor upon the eloquent persuasions or pragmaticals of Mr. Secretary Winwood; but upon them"— meaning himself—who "have so humbled Sir Edward Coke, as he seeketh now that with submission which (as your Majesty knoweth) before he rejected with scorn." And then he says that if the King really wishes for the match, concerning which he should like more definite orders, he will further it; for, says he, "though I will not wager on women's minds, I can prevail more with the mother than any other man."

King James's reply is not in existence, and it is unknown; but, judging from a further letter of Bacon's, it must have been rather cold and unfavourable; and, in Bacon's second letter to the King, he was foolish enough to express a fear lest Buckingham's "height of fortune might make him too secure." In his answer to this second letter of Bacon, James reproves him for plotting with his adversary's wife to overthrow him, saying "this is to be in league with Delilah." He also scolds Bacon for being afraid that Buckingham's height of fortune might make him "misknow himself." The King protests that Buckingham is farther removed from such a vice than any of his other courtiers. Bacon, he says, ought to have written to the King instead of to Buckingham about "the inconvenience of the match:" "that would have been the part of a true servant to us, and of a true friend to him [Buckingham]. But first to make an opposition, then to give advice, by way of friendship, is to make the plough go before the horse."

By the time these letters had been carried backwards and forwards, to and from Scotland and the North of England, a later date had been reached than we have legitimately arrived at in our story, and we must now go back to within a few days of Sir Edward Coke's famous raid at Oatlands.

FOOTNOTES:

[14] *Chief Justices*, Vol. I., pp. 297-298
[15] *S.P. Dom.*, James I., July, 1617. Chamberlain to Sir Dudley Carleton.
[16] Campbell, p. 298.
[17] Lord Campbell's account.
[18] Quoted by Spedding in his *Life of Bacon*.
[19] Foard's *Life and Correspondence of Bacon*, p. 421.

CHAPTER V.

"They've always been at daggers drawing,
And one another clapper-clawing."

Butler's *Hudibras, Hud.*, II, 2.

BACON had scarcely written his first letters to Buckingham and the King, before he had instructed Yelverton, the Attorney-General, to institute a prosecution against Sir Edward Coke, in the Star Chamber, for the riot at Oatlands, which he made out to have been almost an act of war against the King, in his realm.

Her husband having carried away Frances by force, Lady Elizabeth made an effort to recover her by a similar method. Gerrard wrote to Carleton[20] that Lady Elizabeth, having heard that Frances was to be taken to London, determined to meet her with an armed band and to wrest her from Coke's power.

"The Mother she procureth a Warrant from the Counsell Table whereto were many of the Counsellors to take her agayne from him: goes to meete her as she shold come up. In the coach with her the Lord Haughton, Sir E. Lechbill, Sir Rob. Rich, and others, with 3 score men and Pistolls; they mett her not, yf they had there had bin a notable skirmish, for the Lady Compton was with Mrs. French in the Coach, and there was Clem Coke, my Lord's fighting sonne; and they all swore they would dye in the Place, before they would part with her."

Without doubt, it was fortunate for both parties that they did not meet each other. The attempt was a misfortune, as well as a defeat for Lady Elizabeth; for while she failed to rescue her daughter, she also gave her husband a fresh count to bring against her in the legal proceedings which he forthwith instituted:—[21]

"1. For conveying away her daughter clam et secreté. 2. For endeavouring to bind her to my Lord Oxford without her father's consent. 3. For counterfeiting a letter of my Lord Oxford offering her marriage. 4. For plotting to surprise her daughter and take her away by force, to the breach of the King's peace, and for that purpose assembling a body of desperate fellows, whereof the consequences might have been dangerous."

To these terrible accusations Lady Elizabeth unblushingly replied: "1. I had cause to provide for her quiet, Secretary Winwood threatening she should be married from me in spite of my teeth, and Sir Edward Coke intending to bestow her against her liking: whereupon she asked me for help, I placed her at my cousin-german's house a few days for her health and quiet. 2. My daughter tempted by her father's threats and ill usuage, and pressing me to find a remedy, I did compassionate her condition, and bethought myself of this contract with my Lord of Oxford, if so she liked, and therefore I gave it to her to peruse and consider by herself: she liked it, cheerfully writ it out with her own hand, subscribed it, and returned it to me. 3. The end justifies—at least excuses—the fact: for it was only to hold up my daughter's mind to her own choice that she might with the more constancy endure her imprisonment—having this only antidote to resist the poison—no person or speech being admitted to her but such as spoke Sir John Villiers' language. 4. Be it that I had some tall fellows assembled to such an end, and that something was intended, who intended this?—the mother! And wherefore? Because she was unnaturally and barbarously secluded from her daughter, and her daughter forced against her will, contrary to her vows and liking, to the will of him she disliked."

She then goes on to describe, by way of recrimination, Sir Edward Coke's "most notorious riot, committed at my Lord of Argyle's house, where, without constable or warrant, well weaponed, he took down the doors of the gatehouse and of the house itself, and tore the daughter in that barbarous manner from her mother—justifying it for good law: a word for the encouragement of all notorious and rebellious malefactors from him who had been a Chief Justice, and reputed the oracle of the law."

A *State Paper* (*Dom.*, James I., 19th July, 1617, John Chamberlain to Sir Dudley Carleton) tells us what followed. As correspondence with Sir Dudley Carleton will be largely quoted in these pages, this opportunity may be taken of observing that he was Ambassador, at various times, in Savoy, in the Low Countries, and in Venice, that he became one of Charles the First's principal Ministers of State, and that he was eventually created Viscount Dorchester.

"The next day being all convened before the Council, she" [Frances the daughter] "was sequestered to Mr. Attorney, & yesterday, upon a palliated agreement twixt Sir Edward Coke & his lady, she was sent to Hatton House, with order that the Lady Compton should have access to win her & wear her." One wonders whether the last "&" was accidentally substituted for the word "or," by a slip of the pen. In any case to "wear her" is highly significant!

"It were a long story to tell all the passages of this business, which hath furnished Paul's, & this town very plentifully the whole week." [One of the ecclesiastical scandals of that period was that the nave of St. Paul's Cathedral was a favourite lounge, and a regular exchange for gossip.] "The Lord Coke was in great danger to be committed for disobeying the Council's order, for abusing his warrant, & for the violence used in breaking open the doors; to all of which he gave reasonable answers, &, for the violence, will justify it by law, though orders be given to prefer a bill against him in the Star Chamber. He and his friends complain of hard measure from some of the greatest at that Board, & that he was too much trampled upon with ill language. And our friend" [Winwood] "passed not scot free from the warrant, which the greatest there" [Bacon] "said was subject to a *praemunire*, & withal, told the Lady Compton that they wished well to her and her sons, & would be ready to serve the Earl of Buckingham with all true affection, whereas others did it out of faction & ambition."

Bacon might swagger at the Council Board; but in his heart he was becoming exceedingly uneasy. We saw, at the end of the last chapter, that he had received a very sharp letter from the King; and now the royal favourite himself also wrote in terms which showed, unmistakably, how much Bacon had offended him.[22]

"In this business of my brother's that you over-trouble yourself with, I understand from London, by some of my friends, that you have carried yourself with much scorn and neglect both towards myself and my friends, which, if it prove true, I blame not you but myself."

This was sufficiently alarming, and at least as much so was a letter which came from the King himself in which was written:— [23]

"Whereas you talk of the riot and violence committed by Sir Edward Coke, we wonder you make no mention of the riot and violence of them that stole away his daughter, which was the first ground of all that noise."

It is clear, therefore, that if things were going badly for Coke, they were going almost worse for Bacon, who now found himself in a very awkward position both with the King and with Buckingham. Nor was he succeeding as well as he could have wished in his attacks upon Coke. He had made an attack by proceeding against him for a certain action, when a judge; but Coke had parried this thrust by paying what was then a very large sum to settle the affair.

In a letter to Carleton[24] Gerrard says:—

"The Lord Chiefe Justice Sir Ed. Coke hath payd 3500£ for composition for taking common Bayle for some accused of Pyracye, which hath been urged agaynst him since hys fall. And perhaps fearing more such claps; intending to stand out the storme no longer, privately hath agreed on a match with Sir

John Villiers for hys youngest daughter Franche, the mother's Darling, with which the King was acquainted withall and writt to have it done before hys coming backe."

And presently he says:—

"The caryadge of the business hath made such a ster in the Towne as never was: Nothing can fully represent it but a Commedye."

A letter written on the same day by Sir John Finet mentions the projected marriage of Sir Edward Coke's daughter with Sir John Villiers, who would have £2,000 a year from Buckingham, and be left heir of his lands, as he was already of his Earldom, failing the Earl's male issue. He adds that Sir Edward Coke went cheerily to visit the Queen, and that the common people said he would die Lord Treasurer. Such gossip as that must have been anything but amusing to Bacon.

The Coke-Villiers engagement had now become almost, if not quite, a State affair. Nearly three weeks later Sir Horace Vere wrote to Carleton:—[25]

"I hear nothing so much spoken of here as that of Sir John Villiers and Sir Ed. Coke's daughter. My Lady Hatton doth continue stiff against yt, and yesterday I wayted upon my wife to my Lady of Northumberland's. She tould my wife that she gives yt out that her daughter is formmerlie contracted to an other and to such a one that will not be afeard to plead his interest if he be put to yt."

Six days afterwards a third candidate for Frances Coke was talked about. George Gerrard wrote to the same correspondent:—[26]

"The Lady Hatton's daughter to be maryed to one Cholmely a Baronet. Of late here is by all the frendes of my Lady Hatton a Contract published of Her Daughter Frances to the Erle of Oxford which was sent him to Venice: to which he hath returned and answer that he will come presently over, and see her fayre eyes and conclude the what he shall thinke fit for him to doe: I have sent your Lordship Mis Frances Coke's Love Letter to my

THE CURIOUS CASE OF
LADY PURBECK

Lord of Oxford herein concluded: I believe you never read the like: Thys is like to become a grate business: for the King hath shewed himselfe much in advancing thys matter for Sir John Villiers."

He says that Lady Elizabeth offers to give Lord Oxford "besydes her daughter ... ten and thirty hundred pound a year, which will before twenty years passe bee nigh 6000£ a yeare besydes two houses well furnisht. A Greate fortune for my Ld. yett it is doubted wheather hee will endanger the losse of the King's favor for so fayre a woman and so fayre a fortune."

The following is Frances Coke's enclosed "love letter" of which Gerrard believed, as well he might, that Carleton "never read the like." It is evidently the work of Lady Elizabeth:—

"I vow before God and take the Almighty to witness That I Frances Coke Yonger daughter to Sir Ed. Coke late Lord Chiefe Justice of England, doe give myselfe absolutely to Wife to Henry Ven. Viscount Balboke, Erle of Oxenford, to whom I plight my fayth and inviolate vows, to keepe myselfe till Death us do part: And if even I breake the least of these I pray God Damne mee body and soule in Hell fyre in the world to come: And in thys world I humbly Beseech God the Earth may open and Swallowe mee up quicke to the Terror of all fayth breakers that remayne alive. In witness whereof I have written all thys with my owne hand and seald it with my owne seale (a hart crowned) which I will weare till your retourne to make thys Good that I have sent you. And for further witness I here underneath sett to my Name.

"(Signed) FRANCES COKE in the Presence

"of my deare Mother

"ELIZA HATTON.

["*July 10, 1617.*"]

Lady Elizabeth, however, failed to effect the match. Possibly the letter just quoted may have been too strong meat for Oxford. Even her skill in the gentle art of forgery proved unavailing. Whether Oxford had no fancy for the girl, or the girl had no fancy for Oxford, does not appear, and perhaps other causes may have prevented the marriage; but, although he did not marry Frances, he married her first cousin, Lady Diana, daughter of the second Earl of Exeter, a niece of Lady Elizabeth, and, like Frances, both a great heiress and a beautiful woman. Lord Oxford was killed, a few years afterwards, at the siege of Breda in the Netherlands.

Bacon, now thoroughly frightened, both by the King and by Buckingham, began to trim, and before long he turned completely round and used his influence with Lady Elizabeth to induce her to agree to the Sir John Villiers-match. He wrote a letter on the 21st of August to Buckingham, saying that he was doing all he could to further the marriage of Sir John Villiers with Frances Coke. Among other things he said:—

"I did also send to my Lady Hatton, Coke's wife and some other special friends to acquaint them that I would declare, if anything, for the match so that they may no longer account on [my] assistance. I sent also to Sir John Butler, and after by letter to my Lady [Compton] your mother, to tender my performance of any good office toward the match."

To this letter Buckingham sent a very chilling reply, whereupon Bacon, in his anxiety, sent Yelverton in person to try to conciliate Buckingham and the King, enjoining him to lie so hard and so unblushingly as to declare that Bacon had never hindered, but had in "many ways furthered the marriage;" that all he had done had been to check Coke's "impertinent carriage" in the matter, which he wished had "more nearly resembled the Earl of Buckingham's sweet disposition."

Yet after faithfully fulfilling this nefarious errand, Yelverton failed to conciliate Buckingham, for he wrote the following very unsatisfactory report to Bacon:—

"The Earl [of Buckingham] professeth openly against you;" whereas, "Sir Edward Coke, as if he were already on his wings, triumphs exceedingly; hath much private conference with his Majesty, and in public doth offer himself, and thrust upon the King with as great boldness of speech as heretofore."

Things were beginning to look desperate for Bacon! Indeed

it seemed as if affliction were about to "level the mole-hills," not now of Coke's, but of Bacon's pride; "to plough" Bacon's heart and "make it fit for Wisdom to sow her seed, and for Grace to bring forth her increase," blessings which Bacon had so kindly & so liberally promised to Coke in a letter already quoted.

About the middle of August, Chamberlain wrote that Frances Coke was staying with Sir Robert Coke, Sir Edward's son by his first wife, and that Lady Elizabeth was with her all day, to prevent the access of others; but that, finding her friends were deserting her, and that "she struggles in vain" against the King's will, "she begins to come about," and "upon some conditions will double her husband's portion and make up the match and give it her blessing." Presently he says: "But it seems the Lady Hatton would have all the honour and thanks, and so defeat her husband's purpose, towards whom, of late, she has carried herself very strangely, and, indeed, neither like a wife, nor a wise woman."

As Chamberlain says, Lady Elizabeth was determined that, if she had to yield, she would be paid for doing so, and that her husband should obtain none of the profits of the transaction. It was unfortunate that that transaction should be the means of injuring her daughter whom she loved; but it was very fortunate that it might be the means of injuring her husband whom she hated. Her own account of her final agreement to the marriage may be seen in a letter which she wrote to the King in the following year:—[27]

"I call to witness my Lord Haughton, whom I sent twyce to moove the matter to my Lady Compton, so as by me she would take it. This was after he had so fondly broke off with my Lorde of Bukingham, when he ruled your Majestie's favour scarse at the salerie of a 1,000£. After that my brother and sister of Burghly offered, in the Galerie Chamber at Whitehall, theire service unto my Ladie Compton to further this marriage, so as from me she would take it. Thirdly, myselfe cominge from Kingstone in a coach with my Ladie Compton, I then offered her that if shee would leave Sir Edward Cooke I would proceed with her in this marriage."

Although, as Chamberlain had written, Lady Elizabeth was now beginning "to come about," in fact had come about, her faithful friend, Bacon, in his frantic anxiety to regain the favour of Buckingham and the King, ordered her to be arrested and kept in strict though honourable confinement. In fact, to use a modern term, all the actors in this little drama, possibly with the exception of Frances Coke and Sir John Villiers, were prepared, at any moment, "to give each other away." According to Foard,[28] Bacon was, at this time, busily engaged in preparing for the trial of another member of Lady Elizabeth's family, namely her stepmother, Lady Exeter.[29]

By the irony of fate, it happened that the two mortal enemies, Coke and Bacon, acted together in the matter of the incarceration of Lady Elizabeth; for, while the former pleaded for it, the latter ordered it. It was spent partly at the house of Alderman Bennet,[30] and partly at that of Sir William Craven,[31] Lord Mayor of London in the years 1610 and 1618, and father of the first Earl of Craven. In both houses she was doubtless treated with all respect, and she must have occupied a position in them something between that of a paying-guest and a lunatic living in the private house of a doctor—not that there was any lunacy in the mind of Lady Elizabeth. Quite the contrary!

FOOTNOTES:

[20] *S.P. Dom.*, James I., Vol. XCII, No. 101, 23rd July, 1617.

[21] Campbell, Vol. I., p. 300.

[22] Campbell, Vol. I., p. 301.

[23] *Ibid.*, p. 302.

[24] *S.P. Dom.*, James I., Vol. XCII, No. 101, 22nd July, 1617.

[25] *S.P. Dom.*, James I., Vol. XCIII., No. 18, 12th August, 1617.

[26] *S.P. Dom.*, James I., Vol. XCIII., No. 28, 18th August, 1617.

[27] *Life of Sir Edward Coke.* By Humphrey Woolrych. London: J. &

W.T. Clarke, 1826, pp. 146-48.

[28] *Life and Correspondence of Francis Bacon*. London: Saunders, Otley & Co., 1861, p. 459.

[29] She was found innocent, and her accusers, Sir Thomas and Lady Lake, were imprisoned and fined. £10,000 to the King, and £5,000 to Lady Exeter as damages for the libel. A chambermaid who was one of the witnesses, was whipped at the cart's tail for her perjury. Lady Roos, the wife of Lady Exeter's step-grandson, and a daughter of the Lakes, made a full confession that she had participated in spreading the scandal. She was sentenced to be imprisoned during the King's pleasure.

[30] *S.P. Dom.*, James I., Vol. XCIII., 6th October, 1617. Letter from Sir Gerald Herbert.

[31] Campbell, Vol. I., p. 303. fn. The imprisonment of what were called "people of quality" usually took place either in the Tower or in the private houses of Aldermen, in those times, although they were sometimes imprisoned in the Fleet.

CHAPTER VI.

"Of all the actions of a man's life his marriage doth least concern other people; yet of all actions of our life it is most meddled with by other people."

SELDEN.

IN all these negotiations, and caballings, and intriguings, the person most concerned, Frances Coke, the beauty and the heiress, was only the ball in the game. Neither her father nor her mother nor anybody else either considered her feelings or consulted her wishes about the proposed marriage, except so far as it was to their own personal interest to do so.

At last the poor girl yielded, or pretended to yield. Lord Campbell says, as well he may, "and without doubt, just as Frances had before copied and signed the contract with Lord Oxford, at the command of her mother, she now copied and signed the following letter[32] to her mother at the command of her father."

"'MADAM,

"'I must now humbly desire your patience in giving me leave to declare myself to you, which is, that without your allowance and liking, all the world shall never make me entangle or tie myself. But now, by my father's especial commandment, I obey him in presenting to you my humble duty in a tedious letter, which is to know your Ladyship's pleasure, not as a thing I desire: but I resolve to be wholly ruled by my father and yourself, knowing your judgments to be such that I may well rely upon, and hoping that conscience and the natural affection parents bear to

46

children will let you do nothing but for my good, and that you may receive comfort, I being a mere child and not understanding the world nor what is good for myself. That which makes me a little give way to it is, that I hope it will be a means to procure a reconciliation between my father and your Ladyship. Also I think it will be a means of the King's favour to my father. Himself [Sir John Villiers] is not to be misliked: his fortune is very good, a gentleman well born.... So I humbly take my leave, praying that all things may be to every one's contentment.

"'Your Ladyship's most obedient

"'and humble daughter for ever,

"'FRANCES COKE.

"'Dear Mother believe there has no violent means been used to me by words or deeds.'"

This, as Campbell says, has every appearance of being a letter copied from one written by her father. There is also reason for believing that Coke added the postscript for a very special purpose; for the question arises how Frances, who is admitted on all sides to have hated Sir John Villiers, could have been induced to copy and to sign this letter. Was she literally forced to do so? There happens to be an answer to that question.

"*Notes of the Villiers Family.*[33]

"*N.B. I.B.N.* have heard it from a noble Peer, a near relation of the Danvers family, and Mr. Villiers, Brother to the person who now claims the Earldom of Buckingham, as his Brother assumed the Title, that the Lady Frances Viscountess Purbeck was tyed to the Bed-Poste and severely whipped into consent to marry with the Duke of Buckingham's Brother, Sir John Villiers, A° 1617, who was 2 years after created Viscount Purbeck."

This was written after the death of Frances, but it has been accepted as true, and that may well be. It is difficult in our days to believe that a young lady could be put to physical torture by her father, until she consented to marry a man whom she loathed; but the parental ethics of those times were very different from those of our own. A man like Coke would have no difficulty in persuading himself that a marriage with Sir John Villiers would be for his daughter's welfare, and, consequently, that a whipping to bring that marriage about would also be for her welfare.

Coke had often waited for the confessions of men who were in frightful agony on the rack, in the dungeons of the Tower; so it must have been a mere trifle to him to await his daughter's consent to a marriage which she detested, while he whipped her, or watched her being whipped, reflecting upon the luxury of the bed-post in comparison with the agony of the rack, flattering himself that he was acting in obedience to Holy Scripture, and piously meditating upon the gratification he must be giving to the soul of Solomon by this exercise of domestic discipline. But a reader may well wonder whether the old brute considered for a moment the worthlessness of a form of marriage obtained by torture, or the fact that such a so-called marriage could be annulled without difficulty.

Lady Elizabeth, perceiving that her only chance left of winning the game was to over-trump her husband, and recognising that her only hope of freedom and prosperity was by consenting to the wishes of Buckingham and James, wrote to the King himself, to say that she would agree to the marriage and would settle her property on her daughter and Sir John Villiers.

Eventually, "The marriage settlement," says Campbell, "was drawn under the King's own superintendence, that both father and mother might be compelled to do justice to Sir John Villiers and his bride; and on Michaelmas Day the marriage was actually celebrated at Hampton Court Palace, in the presence of the King and Queen and all the chief nobility of England. Strange to say, Lady Hatton still remained in confinement, while Sir Edward Coke, in nine coaches,"—one man in nine coaches!—&brought his daughter and his friends to the palace, from his son's at Kingston-Townsend. The banquet was most splendid: a masque was performed in the evening; the stocking was thrown with all due spirit: and the bride and bride-groom, according to long established fashion, received the company at their couchée."

In a footnote to *The Secret History of James I.*, Vol. I., p. 444,[34] we read:

"The Scottish historian, Johnstone, says that Purbeck's marriage was celebrated amid the gratulation of the fawning courtiers, but stained by the tears of the reluctant bride, who was a sacrifice to her father's ambition of the alliance with Buckingham's family."

Here is another account of the wedding, in a letter[35] from Sir Gerard Herbert to Carleton:—

"Maie it please yor. Lordshippe.

" ... I know not any news to write yor. Lo: other than the marriadge of Sir John Villiers with my Lord Coke's youngest daughter, on Monday last, beynge Michailmas day at Hampton Courte when King Queen and prince were present in the chappell to see them married. My Lord Coke gave his daughter to the Kinge (with some words of complement at the givinge). The King gave her Sir John Villiers. The prince sate with her to grand dynner and supper so to many Lordes and Ladies, my Lord Canterbury, my Lord Treasurer, my Lord Chamberlayne, etc. The King dynner and supper droncke healthe to the bride, the bridgegroome stood behinde the bride; the dynner and supper. The Bride and Bridegroome lay next day a bedd till past 12 a clocke, for the Kinge sent worde he wold come to see them, therefore wold they not rise. My Lord Coke looked with a merrie Countenance and sate at the dynner and supper, but my Lady Hatton was not at the weddinge, but is still at Alderman Bennettes prisonere. The King sent for her to the weddinge, but (she) desired to be excused, sayinge she was sicke. My Lord of Buckingham, mother, brethren, there soynes, and his sisters weare throughout day at Court, my Lord Cooke's sonnes and there soynes, but I saw never a Cecill. The Sonday my Lord Coke was restored to his place of counsellor as before....

"Yo: Lo: in all service to commande

"(Signed) GERRARD HERBERT.

"LONDON, this

"6 Oct."

Lady Elizabeth would not submit to being let out of prison, just for the day, in order to witness the wedding, which was to a large extent a triumph for her husband. She meant, on the contrary, to have a triumph on her own account. Her intention was that one of those who had had a hand in putting her into prison—a prison which in fact was a comfortable house—should come to take her out of it; and she was determined to be escorted from her place of punishment, not as a repentant criminal, but as a conquering heroine.

In a letter to Carleton[36] Chamberlain says:—

"The King coming to towne yesterday it was told me that the Earle of Buck, meant to go himself and fetch 'Lady Elizabeth' as yt were in pomp Fr. William corner (where she hath ben so long committed), and bring her to the King, who upon a letter of her submission is graciously affected towards her. ... Seeing her yielding and as it were won to geve her allowance to the late marriage," the King will "give her all the contentment and countenance he can in hope of the great portion she may bestow upon" Buckingham's brother, Sir John Villiers; "for there is little or nothing more to be looked for from Sr. Ed. Cooke, who hath redemed the land he had allotted his daughter for 20,000£ so that they have already had 30,000£ of him paide down.... She layes all the fault of her late troubles upon the deceased secretarie," Winwood, "who not long since telling her brother that for all her bitter speeches they two [Lady Elizabeth and her husband] shold become goode frends again. She protested she wold sooner be frends with the Devill."

Lady Elizabeth was so much in the King's good graces that aspirants for office tried to win her influence with James and Buckingham in their favour. Chamberlain, in the letter quoted above, expresses the wish that she might endeavour to obtain for Carleton the post of Secretary of State, which had just then fallen vacant through the death of Winwood. In a letter[37] written a fortnight later, however, Chamberlain says:—

"Your father Savile is gon into Kent to his daughter Salley, the day before his goings I met him and wisht him to applie the Lady Hatton, whom he had alredy visited but moved her in nothing because the time was not fit but she meant to do yt before he went. Some whisper that she is alredy ingaged and meanes to employ her full force strength and vertue for the L. Hawton or Hollis, who is become her prime privie Counsailor and doth by all meanes interest and combine her with the Lady of Suffolke and that house. A man whom Sir Edward Cooke can no wayes indure, and from whose company he wold faine but cannot debarre her." Obviously a very sufficient reason for liking him and espousing his cause.

Lady Elizabeth had fairly outwitted her husband; but, as will presently be seen, she had not yet quite done with him. Another account of her liberation is to be found in *Strafford's Letters and Despatches*:—[38]

"The expectancy of Sir Edward's rising is much abated by reason of his lady's liberty, who was brought in great honour to Exeter House by my Lord of Buckingham, from Sir William Craven's, whither she had been remanded, presented by his Lordship to the King, received gracious usage, reconciled to her daughter by his Majesty, and her house in Holborn enlightened by his presence at dinner, where there was a royal feast: and to make it more absolutely her own, express commandment given by her Ladyship that neither Sir Edward Coke nor any of his servants should be admitted."

Here is another account[39] of the same banquet, as well as of one given in return by Buckingham's mother, who was still hoping that Lady Elizabeth would increase Sir John Villiers' allowance:—

"The Lady Hatton's feast was very magnificall and the King graced her every way, and made foure of her creatures knights.... This weeke on wensday [Lady Compton] made a great feast to the Lady Hatton, and much court there is between them, but for ought I can heare the Lady Hatton holdes her handes and gives not" (The original is much torn and damaged here) "out of her milke so fouly [fully] as was expected which in due time may turn the matter about againe.... There were some errors at the Lady Hatton's feast (yf it were not of purpose) that the L. Chamberlain and the L. of Arundell were not invited but went away to theyre owne dinner and came backe to wait on the King and Prince: but the greatest error was that the goodman of the house was neither invited nor spoken of but dined that day at the Temple." Camden's account of this dinner (Ed. 1719, Vol. II., p. 648), although very abrupt, is to the point: "The wife of Sir Ed. Coke *quondam* Lord Chief Justice, entertained the King, Buckingham, and the rest of the Peers, at a splendid dinner, and not inviting her husband."

In a letter to Carlton[40] John Pory said of this dinner: "My Lo. Coke only was absent, who in all vulgar opinions was there expected. His Majesty was never merrier nor more satisfied, who had not patience to sit a quarter of an hour without drinking the health of my Lady Elizabeth Hatton, which was pledged first by my Lord Keeper [Bacon] and my Lord Marquis Hamilton, and then by all the gallants in the next room."

This exclusion from her party was a direct and a very public insult to Coke on the part of his wife, and, through consent, on that of the King also. All Coke had gained by his daughter's marriage with Sir John Villiers was restoration to the Privy Council. As he had made up his mind to take his daughter to market, he should have made certain of his bargain. This he failed to do. As has been shown, he promised £10,000 down with her and £1,000 a year. This Buckingham did not consider enough; but Coke refused to promise more, declaring that he would not buy the King's favour too dear. In a letter to Carleton, Chamberlain says that, if he had not "stuck" at this, Coke might have been Lord Chancellor. As it was, he incurred the whole odium of having sold his daughter, while his wife, who had gained the credit of protesting against that atrocious bargain, quietly pocketed its price in the coin of royal favour. Lady Elizabeth not only embroiled her own family, but also brought discord about her affairs into the family of another, as may be inferred from the following letter:—[41]

"Elizabeth, Lady Hatton, to Carleton.

"MY LORDE,

"I understande by your letter the quarrell of unkindness betweene yourself and your wife, but having considered the cause of the difference to proceed only from your loving respect shewne towards me, I hope that my thankfulle acknowledgements will be sufficient reconcilement to give you both proceedings for the continuance of your wonted goode wille and affectione ... even though I understande by your letter you thinke women to be capable of little else but compliments. Wherefore to express a gracious courtesie for your kindness as in the few wordes I am willing to utter you may assure yourselfe yt my desire is to remayne

"Your assured loving Frend
"(Signed) ELIZA HATTON.

"Hatton House
    "*20th March 1618.*"

One naturally wonders whether, if Carleton showed this letter to his wife, it would tend to heal "the quarrell of unkindness" between them, or to make it worse. Which effect was intended by the writer of the letter is pretty evident. This little epistle might have been written by Becky Sharpe.

FOOTNOTES:

[32] *Coles' MSS.*, Vol. XXXIII. p. 17.
[33] *Coles' MSS.*, Vol. XXXIII., p. 17. (Brit. Museum MSS. No. 5834.)
[34] Longmans & Co., 1811.
[35] *S.P. Dom.*, James I., Vol. XCIII., No. 114, 6th October, 1617.
[36] *S.P. Dom.*, James I., Vol. XCIII., No. 158, 31st Oct., 1617.
[37] *S.P. Dom.*, James I., Vol. XCIV., 15th November, 1617.

[38] Vol. I., p. 5.

[39] *S.P. Dom.*, James I., Vol. XCIV., No. 30, 15th November, 1617. Chamberlain to Carleton.

[40] *S.P.*, XCIV., No. 15.

[41] *S.P. Dom.*, James I., Vol. XCVI., No. 69.

CHAPTER VII.

"What is wedlock forced, but a hell? "

—Henry VI., I., v., 5.

LITTLE is recorded of the early married life of Sir John and Lady Villiers. Before it began they had both been mere pawns in the game, and pawns they remained for a good many years afterwards. If before her marriage the career of Lady Villiers had lain in the hands of her father and her mother; after her marriage it was, for a time, in the hands of her brother-in-law, Buckingham, as the career of Sir John always had been and continued to be during the life of Buckingham.

In the *Secret History of James I.*[42] we read concerning Buckingham: "But I must tell you what got him most hatred, to raise brothers and brothers-in-law to the highest ranks of nobility, which were not capable of the place of scarce a justice of the peace; only his brother, Purbeck, had more wit and honesty than all the kindred beside and did keep him in some bounds of honesty and modesty, whilst he lived about him, & would speake plaine English to him." If this be true, there must have been some good in Sir John; but Buckingham was impervious to his advice and treated him just as he pleased. It is possible, again, that Lady Villiers, without having any of the affection which a wife ought to have for a husband, may have had a sort of respect for him as a man of probity, much older than herself, who treated her well and even kindly.

George Villiers, a mushroom-grown Duke himself, having

made the King create his mother Countess of Buckingham, bethought him of his eldest brother and determined to make him a peer. And not only that. He also conceived the idea of squeezing some more money out of his brother's mother-in-law for him, by offering her a peerage, for the cash thus obtained. It was suggested to her that she might be made Countess of Westmorland; but "she refused to buy the title at the price demanded."[43] Indeed, Lady Elizabeth was ready to fight anybody and everybody. On the one hand, she resisted the attempts of the almighty Buckingham to bleed her still further for Sir John Villiers, and, on the other, she wrote to the King concerning her husband: "I find how desirous he is to rubb up anie thing to make ill bloode betwixt my sonne Villiers & myselfe."[44] Meanwhile she prosecuted her husband in the Star Chamber. Mr. Brant wrote to Carleton: " ... The Ladie Hatton prevayleth exceedingly against her husband and hath driven him into a numnesse of on side, which is a forerunner of ye dead palsie, though now he be somewhat recovured."

In May, 1619, Lady Elizabeth was informed that, if she would give that isle, no longer an island, the Isle of Purbeck, which was her property, to her son-in-law, she should be made Countess of Purbeck and he Viscount Purbeck; but she refused to exchange good land for an empty name. However, in July, Sir John Villiers was created Baron Villiers of Stoke (Stoke Pogis) and Viscount Purbeck. This heaping up of peerages in the Villiers family, in addition to the number of valuable posts, and especially high ecclesiastical posts, obtained by Buckingham for his friends, or for anybody who would bribe him heavily enough to obtain them, led to much murmuring and ill-feeling among those whom he did not thus favour, and greatly irritated the populace. There was no apparent reason why Sir John Villiers should be ennobled, and his peerages were looked upon as a glaring piece of jobbery.

The Court also, at this time, was becoming unpopular. Buckingham was filling it with licentious gallants and with ladies of a type to match them. At Whitehall, there was a constant round of dissipation and libertinism. Besides the very free and easy balls, masques and banquets, there were what were called "quaint conceits" of more than doubtful decency, and there was much buffoonery of a very low type. In the *Secret History of the Court of James I.* it is recorded that, at this time, namely, about 1618 or 1619, there were "none great with Buckingham but bawds and parasites, and such as humoured him in his unchaste pleasures; so that since his first being a pretty, harmless, affable gentleman, he grew insolent, cruel, and a monster not to be endured."

Lord Purbeck held the appointment of Master of the Robes to Prince Charles, and he seems to have lived in the palace of the Prince; for, even as late as 1625, we read of Lady Purbeck remaining in "the Prinses house."[45] In 1620 Chamberlain wrote to Carleton[46] that when Buckingham was overpressed by business, he handed over suitors to his brother Purbeck. On the 18th of January, 1620, a letter[47] of Nethersole's states that Purbeck had resigned his post of Master of the Robes, in order to become Master of the Horse to the Prince.

At some date between that of his marriage in the year 1617 and 1622, Purbeck was received into the Catholic Church, by Father Percy, alias Fisher, a Jesuit. This step does not appear in any way to have affected his position at Court. In a manuscript in the library of the large Jesuit College of Stonyhurst,[48] in Lancashire, it is stated that "the Viscount de Purbeck (sic) brother of the Marquis of Buckingham, having been converted to the Catholic faith and reconciled to the Holy Church, by Father John Persens, S.J., betook himself to the Countess, his mother, and gave her so good an account of the said Father, and of the consolation he had received of him, that she greatly desired to speak to him, and sending him to call the Father, she heard him discourse fully of the Catholic faith, &c."

In *Laud's Diary* there is an entry: "1622, April 23. Being the Tuesday in Easter week, the King sent for me & set me into a course about the countess of Buckingham, who about that time was wavering in point of religion." And again: "May 24. The conference[49] between Mr. Fisher [Percy] a Jesuit, & myself, before the lord Marquis of Buckingham, & the countess, his mother."

There are people who are of opinion that for a Protestant to become a Catholic is an almost certain proof of madness; and such will rejoice to hear that, some time after Lord Purbeck had been received into the Catholic Church, he either showed, or is reputed to have shown, signs of lunacy.

Some authorities doubt whether Purbeck was ever out of his mind; but on the whole the weight of evidence is against them. Yet there are some rather unaccountable incidents in their favour. Again, when anybody is reputed to be mad, exaggerated stories of his doings are very likely to be spread about. Even in these days of advanced medical science, it is sometimes difficult to decide whether a patient is insane or not, and it is quite possible to suffer from very severe fits of depression without being the subject of maniacal melancholia, or from very violent fits of passion without being a madman.

There is just a possibility, too, that Buckingham may have wished to keep his brother quiet, or to get him out of the way, because that brother "would speake plaine English to him" about his licentious conduct and other matters, as we have already read. When a friend or a relative tells a man that he is behaving scandalously, the recipient of the information is apt to say that his informer is "cracked."

The earliest hint of Lord Purbeck's insanity was given in 1620. "The Lord Viscount Purbeck went abroad in the latter end of May 1620, under colour of drinking the waters of Spaw, but in fact, as Camden tells us, to hide his being run mad with pride."[50] The strongest evidence of anything like actual madness is in a letter[51] from Chamberlain to Carleton, written on 8th June, 1622. It may, however, be mere gossip. "The Lord of Purbecke is out of order likewise, for this day feurtnight getting into a roome next the street in Wallingford house, he beat down the glasse windowes with his bare fists and all bloudied &c." If this be true, may it not be possible that he was trying to break his way out of a room in which Buckingham had locked him up on the pretence that he was insane? Of Wallingford House the same correspondent says in another letter: "Buckingham has bought Lord Wallingford's house at Whitehall, by paying some money[52] making Sir Thomas Howard, Visct. Andover, and some say, releasing the Earl and Countess of Somerset."

In August, 1623, the Duchess of Buckingham—this would be Buckingham's wife and not his mother, the Countess of Buckingham—wrote to Conway:—

"SIR,[53]

"My sister and myselfe have seene a letter writt from you to Sir John Keyesley concerning my Brother Purbeck, by his maties command and doubt not but his matie hath bin informed with the most of his distemper. Wee have bin with him the moste parte of this weeke at London, and have found him very temperate by which wee thinke hee is inclining towards his melancholye fitt, which if hee were in, then hee might be perswaded any wayes, which at this instant hee will not, he standeth so affected to the cittee and if there should be any violent course taken with him, wee thinke he would be much the worse, for it, and drive him quite besides himselfe. Therefore wee hould it best to intreat Sir John Keysley and som other of his friends to beare him companie in London and kepe him as private as they can for three or four dayes till his dull fitt be upon him, and then hee may bee had any whither. This in our judgment is the fittest course at this present to be taken with him which we desire you will be pleased to let his Maty. knowe and I shall rest.

"Your assured loving friend,

"(Signed) K. BUCKINGHAM."

From this it would appear either that when Purbeck was in one of his "melancholye fitts," he was quite tractable, but, at other times, he was rather unmanageable; or that, when well, he refused to be ordered about, but when ill, was too poorly to make any resistance. Conway[54] replied as follows:—

"MOST GRATIOUS,

"I have represented to his Matie. your Letter, and he doth gratiously observe those sweete and tender motions which rise in your minde, suitable with your noble, gentle and milde disposition, in which you excell your sex: especially where force or restraint should be done to the brother of youre deare Lorde.

"And I cannot expresse soe finely as his Matie. did, how much he priseth and loveth that blessed sweetness in you, and you in it. But I must tell your Grace his Matie. prays you, not to thinke it a little distemper which carryed him to those publique actes, and publique places, and to consider how irremediable it is, when his intemperance hath carryed him to do some act of dishonour to himselfe, which may, and must, reflect upon his most noble Brother, beyond the follies and disprofits which he dayly practiseth. And that your Grace will not only bee to suffer some sure course to bee taken for the conveying of him into the country, but that you will advise it and assist it with the most gentle (yet sure) wayes possible. That he may be restrayned from the power and possibility of doing such acts as may scorne him, or be dangerous to him: which these wayes of acting can never provide for. For his Matie. sayeth there cannot bee soe much as 'whoe would have thought it,' which is the fooles answere, left for an error in this: for whoe would not thinke that a distempered minde may doe the worst to be done. His Matie. therefore once more prayes you that his former directions to Sir John Ersley may bee put in execution and the safest and surest for the goode of the unfortunate noble person, and honor of youre deare Lorde, his Maties. dearest servant.

"This is that I have in charge. My faith and duty calls for this profession that noe man is more bound to study and endeavour the preservation of the honor and good of those that have interest in my noble patron than myselfe: nor noe man more bound and more ready to obey your commandments than

"Your Grace's most humble servant.

"ALDERSHOT. 30 August 1623."

The chief object aimed at by Conway and, as will be seen presently, by the King, was to prevent any scandal or gossip about Purbeck's behaviour injuring "his Maties. dearest servant," Buckingham. Purbeck's personal interests evidently counted for very little, if for anything.

FOOTNOTES:

[42] P. 444

[43] Woolrych's *Life of Sir Ed. Coke*, p. 150. His authority for this statement is Camden, Ann. Jac., p. 45.

[44] Letter quoted by Woolrych.

[45] *S.P. Dom.*, James I., Vol. CLXXXIII., No. 52.

[46] *S.P. Dom.*, James I., Vol. CXII., No. 1.

[47] *S.P. Dom.*, James I., No. 18.

[48] Stonyhurst MSS., *Angliæ*, Vol. VII. And *Records of the English Province of the Society of Jesus*, Series I., p. 532.

[49] At a subsequent conference King James was present (*Diary of the English College at Rome. The names of the Alumni*, No. 181). Also *Records of the English Province of the S.J.*, Series I., p. 533. The Countess of Buckingham subsequently became a Catholic, and her son, the Duke, obtained leave from the King for Father Percy to "live on parole in her house," which became his home in London for ten years (*Ibid.*, p. 531).

[50] *Biog. Brit.*, notice of Sir E. Coke. Footnote.

[51] *S.P. Dom.*, James I., Vol. CXXXI, No. 24.

[52] *S.P. Dom.*, James I., Vol. CXXVII., No. 35. Chamberlain to Carleton, 19th January, 1622. James I., 1619-23, p. 337. The price paid is said to have been £3,000. See Gardiner, Vol. IV., Chap. XL., p. 279. Lord Wallingford was made Earl of Banbury, and the subsequent claim to this title became as curious as that to the title of Purbeck, which will be shown later.

[53] *S.P. Dom.*, James I., Vol. CLI., No. 86.

[54] *S.P. Dom.*, James I., Vol. CLI., No. 87, 30th August, 1623.

THE CURIOUS CASE OF
LADY PURBECK

CHAPTER VIII.

" ... wed to one half lunatic."

Taming of the Shrew, II., I.

POOR Purbeck seems to have had many amateur keepers. The King gave orders to a Sir John Hippisley to remove him from the Court, in September, 1623; and on the and Sir John wrote to Conway:—[55]

"NOBLE SIR,

"I have received the King's command and your directions in your letters to bring my Lord of Purbecke out of London which I have done and have made no noise of it and have done all I could to give no scandal to the Duke or Viscount: He is now at Hampton Court, but is not willing to go any further till the king send express commande that he shall not staye here.

"Sir I have obeyed all the King's commandes and that without any scandal to the Duke,"—always the point of main importance—"now my humble request to you is that I may be free from entering any farther in this business and that I may come and kiss his Majtes hand for now I am fit.... There is one Mr. Aimes that knoweth my Lord of Purbecke and fitte to be employed by rate he hath power to persuade him. I beseech you grant me fair of this and you shall have it me

"To be your faithfull servant ever to be commanded

"(Signed) JO: HIPPISLEY.

"HAMPTON COURT

"this 2 of *September.*"

From this it is very clear that Hippisley did not want to have anything more to do with a disagreeable business; and the question presents itself whether it was because he disliked acting as keeper to a lunatic, or because he did not think Purbeck so mad as was pretended, if mad at all, and objected to having a hand in a shady transaction.

In the same month, the King wrote himself to Purbeck.[56] The letter is almost illegible; but its purport appears to be to urge Lord Purbeck, out of consideration for Buckingham, as well as for his own good, to go to, and to stay at, whatever place might be appointed for him by the Earl of Middlesex.

During the summer of the following year (1624), Purbeck seems to have recovered his sanity; but only for a time, although a considerable time. Chamberlain wrote[57] to Carleton:—

"My Very Sweete Lord:

" ... The Viscount Purbecke followed the court a good while in very goode temper, and there was speech of making him a marquis that he might go before his younger brother but I heare of late he is fallen backe to his old craise and worse....

"Yor Lops most assuredly

"at command,

"(Signed)   John Chamberlain."

This shows that, if Purbeck was insane, his insanity was intermittent; and it could not have been chronic; for in later years we read that he was managing his own affairs and that he married again, some time after the death of Frances.

From the following letter, written by Lady Purbeck to Buckingham, and unfortunately undated, it would seem that Buckingham had driven her from her home, when she had become the subject of a certain amount of vague scandal, but, so far as was then known, or at least proved, of nothing more; and that he had contrived that she should have none of the wealth which she had brought to her husband. As will be seen, she was apparently penniless, except for what she received from her mother or her friends.

"My Lord[58]:—Though you may judge what pleasure there is in the conversation of a man in the distemper you see your brother in; yet, the duty I owe to a Husband, and the affection I bear him (which sickness shall not diminish) makes me much desire to be with him, to add what comfort I can to his afflicted mind, since his only desire is my company; which, if it please you to satisfy him in, I shall with a very good will suffer with him, and think all but my duty, though I think every wife would not do so. But if you can so far dispense with the laws of God as to keep me from my Husband, yet aggravate it not by restraining me from his means, and all other contentments; but, which I think is rather the part of a Christian, you especially ought much rather to study comforts for me, than to add ills to ills, since it is the marriage of your brother makes me thus miserable. For if you please but to consider, not only the lamentable estate I am in, deprived of all comforts of a Husband, and having no means to live of; besides falling from the hopes my fortune then did promise me; for you know very well, I came no beggar to you, though I am like so to be turn'd off.

"For your own honour and conscience sake, take some course to give me satisfaction, to tye my tongue from crying to God and the world for vengeance, for the unwilling dealing I have received, and think not to send me again to my Mother's, where I have stayed this quarter of a year, hoping (for that Mother said you promised) order should be taken for me; but I never received a penny from you. Her confidence in your nobleness made me so long silent; but now, believe me, I will sooner beg my bread in the streets, to all your dishonours, than any more trouble my friends, and especially my Mother, who was not only content to afford us part of the little means she hath left her, but whilst I was with her, was continually distempered with devised Tales which came from your Family,"—this refers to certain scandalous stories about her own conduct—and withal lost your good opinion, which before she either had, or you made shew of it; but had it been real, I can not think her words would have been so translated, nor in the power of discontented servants' tales to have ended it.

"My Lord, if the great Honour you are in can suffer you to have so mean a thought as of so miserable a creature as I am so made by too much credulity of your fair promises, which I have waited for performance of almost these five years: and now it were time to despair, but that I hope you will one day be yourself, and be governed by your own noble thoughts, and then I am assured to obtain what I desire, since my desires be so reasonable, and but for mine own, which whether you grant or not, the affliction my poor husband is in (if it continue) will keep my mind in a continual purgatory for him, and will suffer me to sign myself no other but your unfortunate sister

"F. PURBECK."

This letter may be taken as evidence of Purbeck's lunacy. On the other hand it might possibly, if not plausibly, be argued that it may only mean that he was in a very bad state of bodily health accompanied by great mental depression. Some readers of these pages may have experienced the capabilities of a liver in lowering the spirits.

As Lady Purbeck says, her mother had now "lost the good opinion" of Buckingham, and undoubtedly this was because she had refused to increase his brother's allowance. So early as 28th November, 1618, John Pary wrote to Carleton,[59] regretting that he had not applied to Lady Bedford to use her influence in order to obtain a certain appointment, instead of applying to Lady Elizabeth, who had fallen out with Buckingham, and now had no influence whatever with him.

Lady Elizabeth, therefore, after having risen by her own skill to be one of the most influential women in England—perhaps the most influential—and that in the face of enormous difficulties, was beginning to fall from her high estate. And besides the bitter disappointment of the loss of influence and of royal smiles, a grievous and humiliating family sorrow was in store for her.

These pages do not constitute a brief on behalf of Lady Purbeck. It is desired that they should do her justice—full justice; but too little is recorded of her personal character to permit any attempt to portray it in detail, or even to make a bold sketch of its principal features. Of her circumstances it is much easier to write with confidence. We have already learned much about them. We have seen that she was brought up in an atmosphere of perpetual domestic discord, ending in a physical struggle between her father and her mother for the possession of her person: that she was afterwards flogged until she consented to make a marriage contract with a man much older than herself, whom she disliked intensely—a form of marriage which was no marriage, as her will for it was wanting and she was literally forced into it, if any girl was ever forced into a marriage.

An old husband hateful to a young wife would become yet more unattractive if he became insane, or eccentric, or even an irritable invalid. Then his change of religion would most likely annoy her extremely. Whether a husband leaves his wife's religion for a better or a worse religion, it is equally distasteful to her.

Her condition would be made still further miserable when she was turned out of her own home, and practically robbed of her own possessions, luxuries and comforts. From what we have seen of her mother, it is difficult to believe that she was a tenderhearted woman, to whom a daughter would go for consolation in her affliction: nor could that daughter place much confidence in a mother who had once deceived her with a forged letter. To her father, who had treated her with great brutality and had sold her just as he might have sold a beast among his farm stock, she would be still less likely to turn for comfort or for counsel. Add to all this that, as the wife of an official in Prince Charles's household, and as the sister-in-law of the reigning favourite, she was a good deal at the Court of James I. at a time when it was one of the most dissolute in Europe; and it will be easy to recognise that her whole life had been spent in unwholesome atmospheres.

When we consider the position of a very beautiful girl of between twenty-one and twenty-four, who had had such an education, had endured such villainous treatment, and was now placed under such trying conditions, we can but feel prepared to hear that some or other of the usual results of bad education, bad treatment, and bad surroundings exhibited themselves, and surely if trouble, and worse than trouble, was ever likely to come of a marriage that had been an empty form, Lady Purbeck's was one after which it might be expected.

And it came! Near Cripple Gate, at the North Wall of London, in October, 1624, was born a boy named Robert Wright. More than a century later the Vicar of the Parish was asked to refer to his registers about this event, and he sent the following reply:—
[60]

"LONDON, *April 10 1740.*

SIR,

"I have searched my Parish Register according to your directions and have found the following Entry concerning Robert Wright.

"Christening in October 1624.

"Robert, Son of John Wright, Gentleman, of Bishopthorpe in Yorkshire, baptised in the Garden House of Mr. Manninge at the upper end of White Cross Street ... 20th.

"I am, Sir,

"Your very humble servant,

"WILL NICHOLLS,

"Vicar of St. Giles's Cripplegate."

The father of this boy was, in reality, Sir Robert Howard, the fifth son of the Earl of Suffolk, the Earl to whose vigilance the discovery of the Gunpowder Plot is attributed by some authorities. But Suffolk had incurred the enmity of Buckingham, had been deprived of the office of Lord Treasurer, had been tried for peculation in the discharge of it, and then condemned in the Star Chamber to imprisonment in the Tower and a fine of £30,000. When he was liberated, he was told that two of his sons, who held places in the King's household, were expected to resign them; but Suffolk, in very spirited letters to the King and to Buckingham (*Cabala*, pp. 333, 334), protested against this. The whole family, therefore, was in bad odour at Court and with Buckingham at this time.

Sir Robert Howard was a brother of the first Earl of Berkshire, who married a niece of Lady Elizabeth Hatton. It may possibly have been through this connection by marriage that Sir Robert Howard became acquainted and intimate with Lady Purbeck; and, to make a long story short, let it be observed here that, in relation to the boy who was christened Robert Wright, Lady Purbeck had had what, among the lower classes, is euphemistically termed "a misfortune."

FOOTNOTES:

[55] *S.P. Dom.*, James I., Vol. CLIII., No. 6.

[56] *S.P. Dom.*, James I., Vol. CLII, No. 13.

[57] *S.P. Dom.*, James I., Vol. CLXX., No. 54, 24th July, 1624.

[58] *Cabala, Sive Scrinia Sacra*, etc., p. 318.

[59] *S.P. Dom.*, James I., Vol. CIII., No. 111.

[60] *Coles' MSS.*, Vol. XXXIII., pp. 17, 18.

CHAPTER IX.

———————

"The first thing we do, let's kill all the lawyers."

Henry VI., 2, IV., 2.

ALTHOUGH Robert Wright was baptised in October, 1624, the date of his birth is uncertain. He may have been born many months before his baptism; but his being christened at a private house rather points the other way. Anyhow, proceedings were instituted against Sir Robert Howard and Lady Purbeck, long before the child was christened. In *The Diary of Archbishop Laud* occurs the following entry for the year 1624:—

"*Januar. 21. Friday.* The business of my *Lord Purbeck*, made known unto me by my Lord Duke." This business of my Lord Purbeck may refer exclusively to his insanity, or reputed insanity; but it seems more probable that it has reference to the Howard-Purbeck scandal.

A letter[61] from the Lord Keeper, Williams, Bishop of Lincoln, to Buckingham, and written on 11th March, 1624, shows that the proceedings against Sir Robert Howard and Lady Purbeck were in full swing at that date.

"May it please your Grace,

"Sir Robert Howard appeared yesterday, and continues obstinate in his refusal to swear. When we came to examine the Commission for our Power to fine him for his Obstinacy, we found, that Sir Edward Coke (foreseeing, out of a prophetical Spirit, how near it might concern a Grand-Child of his own), hath expunged this Clause (by the Help of the Earl of Salisbury) out of the Commission, and left us nothing but the rusty Sword of the Church, Excommunication, to vindicate the Authority of this Court. We have given him day until Saturday next, either to conform, or to be excommunicated. She hath answered wittily, and cunningly, but yet sufficient for the Cognisance of the Court: Confesseth a Fame of Incontinence against her and Howard; but saith, it was raised by her Husband's Kindred. I do not doubt, but the Business will go on well; but (peradventure) more slowly, if Howard continue refractory, for want of this power to fine and amerce him."

That Lady Purbeck "answered wittily," or, as would now be said, "cleverly" in court, is not to be wondered at; for was she not the daughter of a father who had been the cleverest barrister of his day, and of a mother who was more than a match for that cleverest of barristers?

A couple of days later the same correspondent wrote[62] to the Duke: "For your Brother's Business, this is all I have to acquaint your Grace with: Sir Robert Howard appeared, yesterday, at Lambeth, pretended want of Council (the Doctors being out of Town) desired respite until to-morrow, and had it granted by my Lord's Grace. Most men think he will not take his Oath at all; I do incline to the contrary Opinion, because, to my knowledge, he hath sent far and near, for the most able Doctors in the Kingdom, to be feed for him, which were great folly, if he intended not to answer. He is extreamly commended for his closeness and secrecy by the major part of our Auditors (the He and She Good-fellows of the Town,) and though he refuseth to be a Confessor, yet he is sure to dye a Martyr, and most of the Ladies in Town will worship at his Shrine. The Lady Hatton, some nine days since was at Stoke, with the good Knight her Husband, for some counsel in this particular; but he refused to meddle therewithal, and dismist her Ladiship, when she had stayed with him very lovingly half a quarter of an hour."

There had been some sort of reconciliation between Coke and Lady Elizabeth in July, 1621, says Woolrych in his life of Coke, "a reconciliation effected through the mediation of the King." It was not, however, cordial; for "we have good reason to suppose that they lived apart to the day of Coke's death," says Campbell. At any rate they were now on speaking terms, though that was about all; for, as we have just seen, Coke refused to meddle in a matter upon which he was eminently qualified to give an opinion, and he got rid of his wife after an interview of seven minutes and a half, instead of giving her the leisurely and lengthy advice and instructions which were the least that she might have expected from him. Sympathy, of course, she could not have hoped for.

The proceedings against the two delinquents would appear to have been in abeyance during the rest of the year; but in January, 1625, Sir John Coke—the Secretary of State, not one of the Cokes of Sir Edward's family—wrote[63] to Buckingham, saying that the King, although so ill as scarcely to be able to sign his name, had put it to the warrant sent by the Lord Chief Justice for authority to examine into Lady Purbeck's business. This warrant, however, James either issued with certain qualifications, or else privately advised Buckingham only to act upon with prudence, as may be inferred from the following letter,[64] written on February the 11th, by Buckingham to the Lord Chief Justice:—

"I have moved the P. for a warrant from his matie for the commitment of Sir Ro. Howard and my sister Purbeck, but his matie hath out of his gracious and provident care of me dissuaded me in this lest upon it coming to a publique hearing it might be thought that I had gained power more by the way of favour than by the wayes of justice.... I desire you to acquaint this bearer Mr. Innocent Lanier all the particulars of this matter for I know him to be very honest, and discreete and secret." The part of the letter immediately following is illegible, but presently it goes on to say that Lanier[65] is much trusted by his brother Purbeck; that Lanier will not otherwise be able to keep his brother with him; and that, if he leaves, Sir Robert and Lady Purbeck "by their crafty insinuations will draw from him speeches to their advantage."

Now, if Purbeck were still insane, or anything near it, no

"speeches drawn from him" could have had any effect for the advantage of Lady Purbeck and Sir Robert. And it is clear from this letter that Lady Purbeck was even at that time on good terms with her husband and able to influence him. A reader might have been tempted to imagine that Purbeck's "melancholy fitts" of insanity were the result of misery about his wife's infidelity; but, if she could still "draw from him speeches to her advantage," this cannot have been the case. The prosecution of Lady Purbeck was pretty clearly at the instigation of Buckingham and not of Purbeck. There is just a possibility that Purbeck had refused to proceed against her, and that Buckingham represented him as mad in order to act in his place, as his brother, and divorce Lady Purbeck; although such a theory is not supported by strong evidence. There is, however, this evidence in its support, that Purbeck acknowledged the boy christened Robert Wright as his own son some years later.

It is true that, fifty years afterwards, in a petition to the House of Lords[66] by Lord Denbigh against a claim made by a son of Robert Wright, it is stated that Lord and Lady Purbeck had not lived together as man and wife for two years before the birth of Robert Wright; and that Lord Purbeck "was entrusted in the hands of physicians for the cure of a melancholy distemper, occasioned by the cruelty and disorders of his wife." But this claimed absence of two years, or anything approaching two years, is very questionable, if not very improbable; and although there is not much doubt as to the real parentage of Robert Wright, Purbeck may have lived with his wife sufficiently near the birth of the boy to imagine himself his father. Indeed, as the following letter will show, she was so far at Court, as to be living in Prince Charles's house so late as February, 1625, a year after the birth of the boy. Moreover, as we have seen, Lord Purbeck held office in Prince Charles's household, and from this it might be inferred that Purbeck and Lady Purbeck were then together. This is the more likely because in the following letter Buckingham expresses a fear that his "brother will be also every day running to her and give her occasion to worke on him by the subtlty of her discourse." And if the husband and wife had access to each other when the proceedings against the latter had gone so far, they are much more likely to have been together during the year preceding the birth of the boy.

All this only affects the question whether Purbeck discredited his wife's fidelity. Nothing has been said above in favour of the theory that she was faithful.

Buckingham experienced considerable difficulties in the prosecution of Lady Purbeck. On 15th February, 1625, he wrote[67] from Newmarket to the Lord Chief Justice:—

"My Lord,

"I understande you are not yet resolved to committ my sister Purbeck who (if she be at Libbertie) will be still plotting and devising with her ill counsellors to cover and conceal the truth and fowlness of her crime and my brother will be also every day running to her and give her occasion to worke on him by the subtlty of her discourse. It is known that His Matie was tender (at the first mention of this business) of the hande of a Lady of her quallity but sure [if] he hath fully understood the proofs and truth of her fault and how dishonorably she hath carryed herself he would have no more support showen to her than to an ordinary Lady in the like case for that she hath by her ill carriage forfyted that hande."

Things were not going so well now as they had been with Buckingham. Within twelve months he was to be impeached in the House of Commons; and, although still high in the royal favour, his King may not have been so completely his servant at this time as he had been formerly. Buckingham continues:—

"It is likewise very unfit she should remayne in the Prinses house for defying which I thinke much aggravates her crimes and his highness often speaks in distast of her continuance there. You are well acquainted with the proof which is against her, so as I shall not nede to tell you how much it reminds me to be carefull in the prosecution of her faulte but I assure you there is nothing that more sollisits my minde. I ... thanke you for the paynes you have always taken in this business, which my earnest desire is to have to be fully discovered and that you will for much oblige me by the continuance of the care and diligence therein as that she may be tymely prevented in her cunning endeavours to hinder the discovery of the truth of the facts whereof she stands justly accused which (in my opinion) cannot be done but by her present commitment.

"And Sir, I rest,

"Your very loving friend.

"Upon syght of the pregnancy of the proofes and the guiltiness of Sir Rob. Howard and my sister, I desire that you will committ them to prison with little respect, from where I heare Sir Rob. Howard is, for an Alderman's House is rather an honour than disparagement to him and rather a place of entertainment to him than a prison." It will be observed that, although the accused persons had not yet been tried, Buckingham wished them to be put into a place of punishment; a place of mere detention would not satisfy him.

Lanier, who, as Buckingham said in a letter quoted above, was much trusted by his brother, seems to have been trusted by Purbeck without reason, as he was evidently in the employment of Buckingham.

A letter[68] written by Buckingham to Coventry, the Attorney-General, and to Heath, the Solicitor-General, contains the following:—

"I perceive by your paper I have read how much I am beholding, and do also understand by Innocent Larnier and others of the persons themselves and my Lo: Chiefe justice have taken in the business concerning the Lady Purbeck for which I thanke you:... but I did hope you would have more discovered before this.... I desire you to say what you think fitt to be done in the matter of the divorce of my brother and to notify me your opinion thereupon and (if you thinke it fitt to be proceeded in that) what is the speedyest worke that may be taken therein."

It was probably of this letter that Buckingham wrote[69] to
Heath, the Solicitor-General, on 16th February, 1625, from
Newmarket:—

" I have written a letter to yourself and to Mr. Attorney
regarding the business of the Lady Purbeck showing that I desire
you principally only to aggravate her crimes that the Lady by
my humble and your like kind favour may yet be kept in prison,
before the returne to towne, for other my brother who hopes
to be going soune will not be kept from her and she will (if he
should meet with her) so worke on him by her subtilty and that
shee will draw from him something to the advantage of her
dishonourable cause and to her end." Here again is evidence
that Purbeck "will not be kept from" his wife; and that, if they
meet "shee will draw something to the advantage of her" case
in the divorce suit. In what form could this something come? Is
it possible that Buckingham may have thought that she might
induce Purbeck to appear as a witness in her favour? Or that she
might persuade him to stop the suit if he should happen to be
sane enough to do so when it came on?

The next letter has an interest, first, because it shows that
Lady Purbeck's child was really in the custody of Buckingham.
Nominally it was probably in that of Purbeck; but, if Purbeck
as a lunatic was in the custody of Buckingham, what was in
Purbeck's custody would be in Buckingham's custody. Presently,
however, we shall hear of the child being with its mother in her
imprisonment at the house of an Alderman.

Innocent Lanier to Buckingham.[70] "May it please your grace,

"Appon my returne to London, I presently repayred to my Lo:
Chiefe Justice, where I found Mr. Attorney and Mr. Solicitor....
I have heer inclosed fore your Grace ther letter which before it
was sealed they showed mee, being something contrary to their
resolution last nyghte, wch was, to have sent for Sr. Ro: Howard
this morning, and so to comitt him close in the Fleett, but of this
I presume ther letter will give yor. Grace such satisfaction that
I shall need neither to write more of it, nor of what is yett past.

They much desier yor. Grace's coming to towne wch. I hope wilbe speedy as it wilbe materiall. I finde them resolved to deale roundly in this Busnes as yor. Grace desiers and are this morning in the examination of divers witness the better to Inform themselves agaynst my Ladies coming this afternoone. The next Day, they Intend to fall uppon Lambe and Frodsham. My Lady uppon the receipt of my lo: Chiefe Justice letter is something dismayed but resolved to prove a new lodging, and new keepers. The Childe, and Nurse, must remayne with us till farther directions, having nothing more at this present to aquaynt yor. Grace of, wth. my humblest duty I take leave.

"Yor. Grace's most humble and
"obedient Servant,
"(Signed) I. LANIER
"DENMARK HOUSE
"*Feb. 19, 1625.*"

"*Enclosed.* Att. Gen. Coventry and Sol. Gen. Heath to Buckingham.

"Have consulted with Sir Henry Martin on Lady Purbeck's business, and think the best plan would be to have the case brought before the High Commission Court, which can sit without delay, in the vacation, and when the crime is proved there, the divorce can be obtained by ordinary law. Think it unadvisable to send the culprits to prison, as it is unusual for persons of their rank but advise that they may be confined in the houses of Aldermen, where in fact they would probably be more closely restrained than in prison."

The last statement sounds curious; especially as we saw, a few pages ago, that Buckingham wrote: "an Alderman's house is rather an honour than disparagement," and "rather a place of entertainment than a prison."

Buckingham now sought a fresh weapon against his sister-in-law. A couple of scoundrels, mentioned in Lanier's letter, and named Frodsham and Lambe, men suspected of sorcery, offered to give evidence to the effect that Lady Purbeck had paid them to help her to bewitch both Purbeck and Buckingham. On the 16th of February, 1625, Buckingham wrote[71] to Coventry, the Attorney-General:—

"I perceive by the paper I have received how much I am beholding to you and do also understand by Innocent Lanier and others of the paynes [you] and my lo. Chief Justice, have taken in the business concerning the Lady Purbeck for which I thanke you ... but I did hope that you would have some more discovered before this tyme. If Lambe and ffrodsham may escape the one by saying what he did was but jugglinge and the other by seeming to affect to be thought a juggler I believe all that hath been already discovered of the truth of this business will be deluded. I do therefore desire that you will take some sound course with them to make them speake more directly and truly to the point and to bout (?) them from their shifts, for Lambe hath hitherto by such means played mock with the world to preserve himself. I desire you to acquaint Innocent Lanier (who is appointed by my brother to sollicit this business) with all the particulars and publique speeche that he may the better know how to imploy this paynes for the discovering of the knot of this villany. I desire you to say well what is fitt to be done in the divorce of my brother and to notify me your opinions thereon and (if you thinke it fitt to be pursued in this) what is the speediest work that may be taken therein. And you discover the best serving friend.

"I rest, &c.

"Newmarket."

If this was true it would seem that Purbeck himself suspected that he had been bewitched.

Yet on that very same day Buckingham wrote to Heath, the Solicitor-General, expressing his opinion that, unless Lady Purbeck were put in prison, Lord Purbeck would not "be kept from her," which does not look as if he can have been afraid lest she should bewitch him. The letter runs:—

"I have written a letter to yourself and Mr. Attorney concerning the business of the Lady Purbeck which I desire you on whose love to me I principally rely to aggravate and ayre the crimes of that Lady and her dealings with Lambe and the like, so soon as yet she may be before my coming to London committed to some prison for otherwise my brother who hopes to be going hence, will not be kept from her and she will (if he should come to her) so worke on him by her subtilty as that she will draw from him something to the advantage of her dishonourable ends and to his prejudice. Iff ffrodsham and Lambe once feele or be brought to feare their punishment I believe they will unfold much more than they yet have, for it seems they have but boath sported in their examinations, &c."

This letter, again, proves that Lord Purbeck was on good terms with Lady Purbeck, and that Buckingham was striving to keep them apart; and it adds still further support to the theory that it was not Lord Purbeck but Buckingham who was trying to divorce Lady Purbeck, by "aggravating and airing her crimes."

Buckingham himself was suspected of having dealings with Lambe on his own account; for Arthur Wilson says, in his *Life of James I.*:[72] "Dr. Lamb, a man of an infamous Conversation, (having been arraigned for a Witch, and found guilty of it at Worcester; and arraigned for a Rape, and found guilty of it at the King's Bench-Bar at Westminster; yet escaped the Stroke of Justice for both, by his Favour in Court) was much employed by the Mother and the Son," *i.e.*, by the Duke of Buckingham and his mother. If this be true, Buckingham's conduct towards Lady Purbeck, in connection with Lambe, does not seem to have been very straightforward.

Lambe's "favour in Court," however, proved no protection to him in the streets. Whitelock writes[73] in 1632: "This Term the business of the Death of Doctor Lamb was in the King's Bench, wherein it appeared that he was neither Dr. nor any way Lettered, but a man odious to the Vulgar, for some Rumors that went of him, that he was a Conjurer or Sorcerer, and he was quarrelled with in the Streets in London, and as the people more and more gathered about him, so they pelted him with rotten Eggs, Stones, and other riff raff, justled him, beat him, bruised him, and so continued pursuing him from Street to Street, till they were five hundred people together following him. This continued three hours together until Night, and no Magistrate or Officer of the Peace once showed himself to stop this Tumult: so the poor man being above eighty years of age, died of this violence, and no Inquisition was taken of it, nor any of the Malefactors discovered in the City."

On the 26th of February Chamberlain wrote[74] to Carleton:—

"The Lady Purbecke wth her young sonne, and Sr. Robert Howard are committed to the custodie of Generall Aldermen Barkham and Freeman to be close kept. When she was carried to Sergeants ynne to be examined by the new L. Chiefe Justice and others she saide she marvailled what those poore old cuckolds had to say to her. There is an imputation laide on her that with powders and potions she did intoxicate her husbands braines, and practised somewhat in that kinde upon the D. of Buckingham. This (they say) is confest by one Lambe a notorious old rascall that was condemned the last sommer at the Ks. bench for a rape and arraigned some yeare or two before at Worcester for bewitching my L. Windsor ... I see not what the fellow can gaine by this confession but to be hangd the sooner. Would you thinke the Lady Hattens stomacke could stoupe to go seeke her L. Cooke at Stoke for his counsaile and assistance in this business?"

It would appear that Buckingham really believed Lady Purbeck to have possessed herself of some powers of witchcraft and that he felt considerable uneasiness on his own account, as well as on his brother's, in connection with it; for he seems to have consulted some other sorcerer, with the object of out-witching the witchery of Lady Purbeck. In some notes[75] by Archbishop Laud for a letter to Buckingham, the following cautious remarks are to be found:—

"I remember your Grace when I came to you on other busyness told me you were gladd I was come, for you were about to send for me, that you calld me asyde into the gallerye behind yorlodgings bye the back stayres. There you told me of one that had made a great offer of an easy and safe cure of your G. brother the Ld. Purbecke.

"That it much trobbled you when he did but beginne to express himselfe because he sayde he would doe it bye onlye touchinge his head with his hands[76] wch made yor Grace jealous in as much as he mentioned noe Naturall Medicine.

"Upon this yor Gr. was pleased to aske what I thought of it. I answered these were busynesses which I had little looked into. But I did not believe the touch of his hand, or any mans els could produce such effects.

"Your G. asked farther if I remembered whether you might not entertayne him farther in discourse to see whether he would open or express any unlawfull practises; wch I thought you might for it went no farther than discourse.

"And to mye remembrance your Grace sayde that he offered to laye his hand on your head sayinge, I would doe noe more than thiss; And that thereupon you started backe, fearinge some sorcerye or ye like, and that you were not quiett till you had spoken with me about it. This, or much to this effect is the uttermost I can remember that passed at ye time."

Buckingham had evidently felt some scruples about meddling with the Black Art, and had consulted Laud on the question. It is also pretty plain that Laud was anxious not to offend Buckingham, yet, at the same time, wished to guard against any possibility of being accused of approving, or even of conniving at, witchcraft. These notes occur in a "draft of a speech, in the handwriting of Bishop Laud, and apparently intended to be addressed to the House of Commons, by the Duke of Buckingham. It has not been found that this latter speech was ever actually spoken."

So far as accusations against Lady Purbeck of witchcraft were concerned, Buckingham must have found that he had no case; for, in a letter[77] to Carleton, written on 12th March, 1625, Chamberlain says that the charge of sorcery had been dropped; but that Lady Purbeck was to be prosecuted for incontinency. He adds that Sir Robert Howard was a close prisoner in the Fleet in spite of the advice given by the Attorney-General and the Solicitor-General three weeks earlier—and that Lady Purbeck was a prisoner at Alderman Barkham's, had no friends who would stand bail for her, and was asking Buckingham to let her have a little money with which to pay her counsel's fees. Eleven days later Chamberlain again wrote[78] to Carleton, saying that Lady Purbeck was acquitting herself well in the Court of High Commission; that a servant of the Archbishop's had been committed for saying that she had been hardly used, and that she called this man one of her martyrs. He also states that Sir Robert Howard had been publicly excommunicated at St. Paul's Cross, for refusing to answer.

How long the delinquents were kept in captivity is very doubtful. Little else is recorded of either of them during the next two years; but, at the time of their trial in 1627, they would seem to have been at liberty. The reason of this long interval between the trial in the Court of High Commission in 1625 and that before the same Court in 1627 seems inexplicable.

FOOTNOTES:

[61] *Cabala*, p. 281.

[62] *Cabala*, p. 282.

[63] *S.P. Dom.*, James I., Vol. CLXXXII, No. 79.

[64] *S.P. Dom.*, James I., Vol. CLXXXIII, No. 41

[65] Innocent Lanier was one of the King's musicians.

[66] *MSS. of the House of Lords*, 228, 30th April, 1675. *Hist. Com. MSS.*, Ninth Report, Part II., p. 50.

[67] *S.P. Dom.*, James I., Vol. CLXXXIII, No. 52.

[68] *S.P. Dom.*, James I., Vol. CLXXXIII, No. 65, 16th February,

1625.

[69] *Ibid.*, No. 66.

[70] *S.P. Dom.*, James I., Vol. CLXXXIV., Nos. 7 and 7.1.

[71] *S.P. Dom.*, James I., Vol. CLXXXIII, No. 65.

[72] *Camden, Complete History of England*, Vol. II., p. 791 (ed. 1719).

[73] *Memorials of the English Affairs*, etc., p. 17.

[74] *S.P. Dom.*, James I., Vol. CLXXXIV., No. 47.

[75] *S.P. Dom.*, Charles I., Vol. XXVI., No. 30.

[76] This looks like an anticipation of Mesmer.

[77] *S.P. Dom.*, James I., Vol. CLXXXV., No. 48.

[78] *S.P. Dom.*, James I., No. 99.

CHAPTER X.

"Let us give great Praise to God, and little Laud to the Devil."

(Grace said by the Court Jester, Archie Armstrong, when he had
begged to act as chaplain, in the absence of that official, at the
dinner-table of Charles I. Archbishop Laud was little in stature.)

THE following account of the trial of Lady Purbeck in 1627 is
given by Archbishop Laud:—[79]

"Now the Cause of *Sir Robert Howard* was this: He fell
in *League* with the *Lady Viscountess Purbeck.* The *Lord Viscount
Purbeck* being in some weakness and distemper, the Lady used
him at her pleasure, and betook her self in a manner, wholly to
Sir Robert Howard, and had a Son by him. She was delivered
of this Child in a Clandestine way, under the Name of *Mistress
Wright.* These things came to be known, and she was brought
into the *High-Commission,* and there, after a Legal Proceeding,
was found guilty of *Adultery,* and sentenced to do *Pennance*:
Many of the great Lords of the Kingdom being present in Court,
and agreeing to the Sentence."

A marginal note states that there were present Sir Thomas
Coventry, the Lord Keeper of the Great Seal, the Earls of
Manchester, Pembroke, Montgomery and Dorset, Viscount
Grandison, five Bishops, two Deans and several other dignitaries,
clerical and legal.

Laud continues: "Upon this Sentence she withdrew her-self,
to avoid the Penance. This Sentence passed at *London-House,* in
Bishop *Mountains* time, *Novemb. 19. An. Dom. 1627.* I was then

present, as Bishop of *Bath* and *Wells*."

The sentence in question was that Lady Purbeck was to be separated from her husband, and that she should do penance, bare-footed, and clad in a white sheet, in the chapel of the Savoy; but a decree of divorce was not given.

No attempt shall be made here to excuse or palliate the sins of Lady Purbeck; but it may be observed in relation to Laud's mention of her having been found guilty of adultery by the Court, that, although she might be guilty of that offence according to the civil law, she was not guilty of it morally; because her so-called marriage was no marriage at all, since she was forced into it against her will.

It cannot be a matter for surprise that Lady Purbeck "withdrew herself" rather than do penance, barefooted, in a white sheet in a fashionable church, and before a crowded congregation, for a crowd there would certainly have been to enjoy the spectacle of the public penance of a Viscountess. For some time her place of withdrawal or, to speak plainly, her place of hiding, was undiscovered. As we have seen, she was sentenced on the 19th of November. She was not arrested; but she was commanded to "present herself" on a certain Sunday at the Savoy chapel, to perform her public penance. As might have been expected, she did not present herself, to the great disappointment of a large congregation, and she thereby exposed herself to arrest. The officials did not discover her place of retreat until about Christmas. The following story of an incident that then happened in connection with this matter is told by Sir John Finett.[80]

A serjeant-at-arms, accompanied by other officers of justice and their men, proceeded to the house in which Lady Purbeck was concealed, and at once guarded every door into the street; but admittance was refused, and the Countess of Buckingham sent "a gentleman" to the "Ambassador of Savoy," whose garden adjoined that of the house in which Lady Purbeck was staying, to beg the Ambassador that he would allow the officers to pass through his house and garden into the garden of Lady Purbeck's house of refuge "for her more easy apprehension and arrest that way."

The Ambassador refused, considering it an indignity to be asked to allow men of such a type a free passage through his house, and feeling horrified at the idea of lending assistance to "the surprise and arrest of a fair lady, his neighbour." After many protests, however, he consented to the entrance of one constable into his garden, and the man was to avail himself of an opportunity which, said the Ambassador, would occur at dinner-time, of passing into the garden of the next house and arresting Lady Purbeck.

In the meantime the Ambassador called his page, "a handsome fair boy," and, with the help of his attendants, dressed him in women's clothes. He then ordered his coach to be brought round, and when it came, his attendants, ostentatiously, but with a show of great hurry and fear of discovery, ran out of the house with the sham-lady and "thrust her suddenly into" the carriage, which immediately drove off.

The constable, congratulating himself upon his sharpness in discovering, as he thought, the escape of Lady Purbeck, at once gave the alarm to his followers outside. The coach "drove fast down the Strand, followed by a multitude of people, and those officers, not without danger to the coachman, from their violence, but with ease to the Ambassador, that had his house by this device cleaned of the constable."

While all this turmoil was going on in the Strand, Lady Purbeck went quietly away to another place of hiding; but her escape got the gallant and kind-hearted Ambassador into great trouble. Buckingham was enraged when he heard of the trick. Sir John Finett shall himself tell us what followed. Buckingham, he says, declared that "all this was done of designe for the ladies escape, (which in that hubbub she made), to his no small prejudice and scorn, in a business that so nearly he said concerned him, (she being wife to his brother), and bringing him children of anothers begetting; yet such as by the law (because begotten and born while her husband was in the land) must be of his fathering.

"The ambassador for his purgation from this charge, went immediately to the Duke at Whitehall, but was denied accesse: Whereupon repairing to my Lord Chamberlain for his mediation, I was sent to him by his lordship, to let him know more particularly the Duke's displeasure, and back by the ambassador to the Duke with his humble request but of one quarter of an hours audience for his disblaming. But the duke returning answer, that having always held him so much his friend and given him so many fair proofs of his respects, he took his proceeding so unkindly, as he was resolved not to speak with him. I reported this to the ambassador, and had for his only answer, what reason cannot do, time will. Yet, after this the Earls of Carliel and Holland interposing; the ambassador, (hungry after his peace from a person of such power, and regarding his masters service and the public affairs), he a seven night after obtained of the duke an interview in Whitehall garden, and after an hours parley, a reconciliation."

As has just been seen, the officers of the law lost sight of Lady Purbeck. So also, for the present do we; but we know what became of her; for she was taken by Sir Robert Howard to his house at Clun, in the extreme south-west of Shropshire, where a small promontory of that county is bordered by Montgomeryshire, Radnorshire and Herefordshire. It is probable that, so long as she was far away from the Court and from London, Buckingham and the authorities took no trouble to find her or her paramour, and almost connived at their escape.

During their absence from our view, it may add to the interest of our story to observe the conditions at that time of some of the other characters who have figured in it, and to consider certain circumstances of the period at which we are halting. Looking back a little way, we shall find that King James, who we noticed was so ill as to be only just able to sign an order connected with the proceedings against Lady Purbeck, died in March, 1625, and that the very correct Charles I. was King during the subsequent proceedings.

Going further back still, we find that Bacon, who had succeeded in overthrowing Coke, was himself overthrown in 1621, three years after the marriage of Coke's daughter to Sir John Villiers, and shortly after Bacon himself had been created Viscount St. Albans. Bacon was impeached on charges of official corruption, and his old enemy, Sir Edward Coke, who was then a member of Parliament, was to have had the pleasure of conducting the impeachment. Coke, however, was deprived of that gratification by Bacon's plea of Guilty, and was obliged to content himself with attending the Speaker to the bar of the House of Lords when judgment was to be prayed, and with hearing the Chief Justice, by order of the Lords, condemn Bacon to a fine of £40,000, incapacity ever to hold any office again, exile from Court, and imprisonment in the Tower during the King's pleasure.

It was generally supposed that the exultant Coke would now be offered the Great Seal; but, to the astonishment of the world and to Coke's unqualified chagrin, the King proclaimed Williams, "a shrewd Welsh parson," as Lord Campbell calls him, Lord Keeper in the place of Bacon. After this disappointment, Coke became even fiercer against the Court than he had been before Bacon's disgrace. Bacon's fine was remitted, "the King's pleasure" as to the length of his imprisonment was only four days, he was allowed to return to Court, and he was enabled to interest himself with the literary pursuits which he loved better than law and almost as much as power; but he was harassed by want of what, perhaps, he may have loved most of all, namely money, and he died in 1626, five years after his fall and condemnation.

Although Buckingham was at the summit of his glory, everything did not go well with him during the period at which he was scheming to rid his brother of Lady Purbeck. In 1623 he went to Spain with Prince Charles to arrange a marriage with the Infanta, a match which he failed to bring about. In 1626 he was impeached, though unsuccessfully, by the House of Commons. In 1627 he commanded an expedition to the Isle of Rhé against the French, on behalf of the Huguenots, and completely failed in the attempt. In 1628 a new Parliament threw the blame upon him of all the troubles and drawbacks from which the country was then suffering; and, in August, the same year, he was murdered by an assassin less than twelve months after he had succeeded in his proceedings against Lady Purbeck.

It was not until shortly after the death of Bacon that his rival, Sir Edward Coke, reached the zenith of his fame as a politician. Only a few months before the death of Buckingham, Coke framed the celebrated Petition of Rights, a document which has often been spoken of as the second *Magna Charta*. He had gained little through his attempt to bribe Buckingham by giving his daughter and her wealth to Buckingham's brother, and he was now exasperated against the royal favourite and that favourite's royal master. "In the House of Commons, Sir Ed. Coke," says Whitelock in his *Memorials*[81] "named the Duke to be the cause of all their miseries, and moves to goe to the King, and by word to acquaint him." Rushworth writes[82] more fully of this speech of Coke's. "Sir Edward Cook spake freely.... Let us palliate no longer; if we do, God will not prosper us. I think the Duke of Buckingham is the cause of all our miseries; and till the King be informed thereof, we shall never go out with honour, or sit with honour here; that man is the Grievance of Grievances: let us set down the causes of all our disasters, and all will reflect upon him." And Coke was as bitter against the King. A little later Charles I. had issued a warrant for a certain commission, when, in a conference with the Lords, Coke moved[83] "That the Warrant may be damned and destroyed."

After the prorogation of Parliament which soon followed, Coke retired into private life and lived at Stoke Pogis, where he is supposed to have encouraged his neighbour, Hampden, in his plots against the Court.

In the year 1632 Lady Purbeck left Sir Robert Howard to live with and take care of her father. She probably went to him on hearing that he had been seriously hurt by a fall from his horse.

In his diary[84] Coke thus describes this accident: "The 3rd of May, 1632, riding in the morning in Stoke, between eight and nine o'clock to take the air, my horse under me had a strange stumble backwards and fell upon me (being above eighty years old) where my head lighted near to sharp stubbles, and the heavy horse upon me." He declares that he suffered "no hurt at all;" but, as a matter of fact, he received an internal injury.

Lord Campbell says that, from this time "his only domestic solace was the company of his daughter, Lady Purbeck, whom he had forgiven,—probably from a consciousness that her errors might be ascribed to his utter disregard of her inclinations when he concerted her marriage. She continued piously to watch over him till his death."

Lady Elizabeth was never reconciled to her husband. On the contrary, she seems to have been very anxiously awaiting his death in order to take possession of Stoke Pogis. Garrard, in a letter[85] to Lord Deputy Strafford written in 1633, says: "Sir Edward Coke was said to be dead, all one morning in Westminster Hall, this term, insomuch that his wife got her brother, Lord Wimbledon, to post with her to Stoke, to get possession of that place; but beyond Colebrook they met with one of his physicians coming from him, who told her of his much amendment, which made them also return to London; some distemper he had fallen into for want of sleep, but is now well again." Lady Elizabeth's keen disappointment may be readily imagined.

It is not likely that the couple of years spent by Lady Purbeck with her father can have been very pleasant ones. He was bad-tempered, ill-mannered, cantankerous and narrow-minded, and he must also have been a dull companion; for beyond legal literature he had read but little. Lord Campbell says: "He shunned the society of" his contemporaries, "Shakespeare and Ben Jonson, as of *vagrants* who ought to be set in the stocks, or whipped from tithing to tithing."

Nor can Lady Purbeck have found him a very tractable patient. He had no faith in either physicians or physic. Mead wrote[86] to

Sir Martin Stuteville: "Sir Edward Coke being now very infirm in body, a friend of his sent him two or three doctors to regulate his health, whom he told that he had never taken physic since he was born, and would not now begin; and that he had now upon him a disease which all the drugs of Asia, the gold of Africa, nor all the doctors of Europe could cure—old age. He therefore both thanked them and his friend that sent them, and dismissed them nobly with a reward of twenty pieces to each man." Doubtless a troublesome invalid for a daughter to manage.

At last it became apparent that the end was rapidly approaching, and then Lady Purbeck was subjected to a most embarrassing annoyance. Two days before her father's death she was summoned from his bedside to receive Sir Francis Windebank, the Secretary of State, who had arrived at the house, accompanied by several attendants, bringing in his hand an order from the King and Council to search Sir Edward Coke's mansion for seditious papers and, if any were found, to arrest him.

Sir Francis, on hearing the critical condition of Sir Edward, assured Lady Purbeck that he would give her father no personal annoyance; but he insisted on searching all the rooms in the house except that in which Coke was lying; and he carried away every manuscript that he could find, including even Sir Edward's will—a depredation which subsequently caused his family great inconvenience. It is believed that Coke was kept in ignorance of this raid upon his house, probably by the care and vigilance of Lady Purbeck. Thus his last hours were undisturbed, and on the 3rd of September, 1634, in the 83rd year of his age, died one of the most disagreeable men of his times, but the most incorruptible judge in a period of exceptional judicial corruption.

FOOTNOTES:

[79] *The History of the Troubles and Tryal of the most Reverend*

Father in God, and Blessed Martyr, William Laud, Archbishop of Canterbury. Wrote by Himself, during his Imprisonment in the Tower: London, R. Chiswell, 1695, p. 146.

[80] *Finetti Philoxenis*, London, 1636, p. 239.

[81] P. 10.

[82] *Historical Collections*, p. 607 (ed. 1659).

[83] Rushworth's *Collections*, p. 616.

[84] Campbell, Vol. I., p. 334.

[85] *Strafford Letters*, I., p. 265.

[86] Harleian MS. 390, fol. 534.

CHAPTER XI.

———————————

"The circle smil'd, then whisper'd, and then sneer'd,
The misses bridled, and the matrons frown'd;
Some hoped things might not turn out as they fear'd:
Some would not deem such women could be found,
Some ne'er believed one half of what they heard:
Some look'd perplex'd, and others look'd profound."
Don Juan, ix., 78.

Soon after the death of Sir Edward Coke, up to the date of which event his daughter had apparently been taking care of him with great filial piety for two years and living a virtuous life, she came to London. About this coming to London Archbishop Laud must be allowed to have his say,[87] albeit not altogether a pleasant say:—

"They," *i.e.*, Sir Robert Howard and Lady Purbeck, "grew to such boldness, that he brought her up to London and lodged her in Westminster. This was so near the Court and in so open view, that the King and the Lords took notice of it, as a thing full of Impudence, that they should so publickly adventure to outface the Justice of the Realm, in so fowl a business. And one day, as I came of course to wait on his Majesty, he took me aside, and told me of it, being then Archbishop of Canterbury; and added, that it was a great reproach to the Church and Nation; and that I neglected my Duty, in case I did not take order for it. I made answer, she was a Wife of a Peer of the Realm; and that without his leave I could not attach her; but that now I knew his Majesty's pleasure, I would do my best to have her taken, and brought to Penance, according to the sentence against her. The next day I had the good hap to apprehend both her and Sir Robert; and by order of the High-Commission-Court, Imprisoned her in the Gate-House and him in the Fleet. This was (as far as I remember) upon a Wednesday; and the Sunday sevennight after, was thought upon to bring her to Penance. She was much troubled at it, and so was he."

In the *Strafford Papers*[88] there is a letter to the Lord Deputy from Garrard, in which he says that, after Lady Purbeck's sentence some years earlier, she had evaded it by flight and had "not been much looked after since;" but that "this winter she lodged herself on the Water side over against Lambeth, I fear too near the road of the Archbishop's barge; whereof some complaint being made, she had the Sergeant at Arms sent with the warrant of the Lords and the Council to carry her to the Gate-House, whence she will hardly get out until she hath done her penance. The same night was a warrant sent signed by the Lords, to the Warden of the Fleet, to take Sir Robert Howard at Suffolk House, and to carry him to the Fleet; but there was never any proceeding against him, for he refused to take the oath *ex-officio*, and had the Parliament to back him out, but I fear he will not escape so now."

It is open to those who may like to do so to take Laud's words as meaning that Lady Purbeck and Sir Robert Howard were again living together in immorality. Possibly that may have been Laud's meaning. If it was, he may have been mistaken. The world is seldom very charitable and, when Sir Robert and Lady Purbeck were both in London—which was comparatively a small place in those days—the gossips would naturally put the worst construction on the matter. If the very proper Charles I. heard such rumours, he would most likely believe them; so also would Laud.

From the meagre evidence existing on the question, there is much—the present writer thinks most—to be said in favour of the theory that the relations of Lady Purbeck to Sir Robert Howard were, at this time, perfectly innocent, and that they had been so ever since she had left him to live with her father, two years earlier. To begin with, is it likely that if, after so long a separation, the pair had wished to resume their illicit intercourse, they would have chosen London as the place in which to do so? Sir Robert may, or may not, have obtained for Lady Purbeck her lodging. If he did, there was not necessarily any harm in that.

Then the fact of Lady Purbeck's returning openly to London looks as if she was conscious of innocence since she had left Sir Robert a couple of years earlier, and as if she believed that the innocence of her recent life was generally known. And, indeed, she might naturally suppose that because, as Garrard wrote, she "had not been much looked after" by the authorities, when she had gone into the country to continue her offence many years earlier, she was perfectly safe in returning to London now that she was living a life of virtue.

Sir Robert Howard, says Garrard's letter, was sought for and taken at Suffolk House, the London home of his brother, whereas Lady Purbeck was taken at, and living at, a house "on the Water side, over against Lambeth." This does not absolutely prove that they were not living together; but it is certainly evidence in that direction.

Again, although it is possible that the King and Laud may have believed in the revival of the criminal intercourse between Lady Purbeck and Sir Robert, it is equally possible that they did not, and that they merely considered it "boldness" and a "thing full of Impudence" to "publickly adventure to outface the Justice of the Realm," when a woman under sentence to do public penance for grave immorality—a woman who had fled to a remote part of the country to escape from that penance—came back to London and took up her quarters "so near the Court, and in so open view," as if nothing had happened; and that, as the sentence had never been repealed, they thought it ought to be executed.

It might even be contended that the conduct of the King and Laud looks in favour of the innocence of Lady Purbeck, at that time; for, if they had had any evidence of a fresh offence, far from being content with executing the sentence for the old transgression, they would probably, if not certainly, have prosecuted her again for the new one, and have either added to the severity of the first sentence, or passed a second to follow it, as a punishment for the second crime.

Be all this as it may, one thing is certain, namely, that the King and Laud were determined to carry out the sentence which had been passed some seven or eight years earlier, now that the escaped convict had had what Laud calls the "Impudence" to come to the capital; and it appears that Sir Robert was to be proceeded against in the Star Chamber upon the old charge.

Apart from any concern on his own account, Sir Robert was greatly distressed that Lady Purbeck should be exposed to public punishment for an offence of the past, of which he himself was at least equally guilty. In the hope of saving her from it, he took into his counsel " Sir ... of Hampshire," some friend whose name is illegible in Laud's MS.

We must now turn attention, for a little time, elsewhere. The first Earl of Danby was a man of great respectability, and he had distinguished himself in arms, both on sea and on land. He was a Knight of the Garter and the Governor of Guernsey, and he had been Lord President of Munster. He had always done those things that he ought to have done, with as great a regularity as his attainted elder brother, Sir Charles Danvers, had done those things that he ought not to have done.

This paragon of a bachelor, at the age of sixty-two, received a visit at his Government House in Guernsey from a youth who requested a private interview. This having been granted, the boy, to the astonishment of Lord Danby, proclaimed himself to be his Lordship's cousin, Frances, Lady Purbeck.[89]

In a former chapter we saw that Lady Purbeck had escaped from punishment through the medium of a boy dressed up like a woman. The process had now been reversed: for she had escaped from the Gate-House—a woman dressed up like a boy. The Sir Somebody Something of Hampshire, says Laud, "with Money, corrupted the Turn-Key of the Prison (so they call him) and conveyed the Lady Forth, and after that into France in Man's Apparel (as that Knight himself hath since made his boast). This was told me the Morning after the escape: And you must think, the good Fellowship of the Town was glad of it." Lady Purbeck, however, did not go first into France. As we have seen, she went to Guernsey and placed herself under the protection of her old cousin, Lord Danby.

That old cousin must have wished devoutly that she had placed herself anywhere else. For the Governor of one of the King's islands to receive and to shelter a criminal flying from justice was a very embarrassing position. On the other hand, to refuse protection to a helpless lady, and that lady a kinswoman, much more to betray her into the hands of her enemies, would have been an act from which any honourable man might well shrink. The possibility that it might be discovered in the island that he was entertaining a woman in male attire must also have been an annoying uncertainty to the immaculate Governor of Guernsey. Over the details of this perplexing situation history has kindly thrown a veil; indeed, we learn nothing further about Lady Purbeck's proceedings until we read, in the already noticed letter of Garrard's, that she landed at St. Malo, whence she eventually went to Paris.

It seems safe to infer that whatever protection and hospitality her relative, Lord Danby, may have afforded to Lady Purbeck, he was heartily glad to get rid of her. If she had originally intended to go to Paris, she would scarcely have made the long voyage of nearly two hundred miles out of her way to Guernsey, and the most natural explanation of that voyage is that she had hoped and expected to obtain concealment, hospitality, and a refuge in the house of her relative. Instead of conceding her these privileges for any length of time, Lord Danby evidently speeded the parting guest with great celerity.

While all this was going on, Sir Robert Howard remained under arrest in London. Laud, writing of Lady Purbeck's escape, says: "In the mean time, I could not but know, though not perhaps prove as then, that Sir Robert Howard laboured and contrived this conveyance. And thereupon in the next sitting of the High-Commission, Ordered him to be close Prisoner, till he brought the Lady forth. So he continued Prisoner about some two or three months."

It may be observed here that some years later, in fact in the year 1640, Sir Robert Howard turned the tables upon Laud for this transaction. "On Munday, December 21," wrote Laud in 1640, "upon a Petition of Sir Robert Howard, I was condemned to pay Five Hundred Pounds unto him for false Imprisonment. And the Lords Order was so strict, that I was commanded to pay him the Money presently, or give Security to pay it in a very short time. I payed it, to satisfie the Command of the House: but was not therein so well advised as I might have been, being Committed for Treason." Laud was at that time a prisoner in the Tower, only to leave it for execution. In addition to this £500, Sir Robert was ordered to have a fine of £250 paid to him by the sorcerer, Lambe, and another fine of £500 by a man named Martin;[90] so altogether, the Long Parliament assigned him,£1,250 damages.

In a letter to the Lord Deputy, dated 24th June, 1635,[91] Garrard says: "Sir Robert Howard, after one month's close imprisonment in the Fleet, obtained his liberty, giving £2,000 bond never more to come at Lady Purbeck, wherein he stands bound alone; but for his appearance within 30 days, if he be called, two of his brothers stand bound for him in £1,500, so I hope there is an end of the business."

On the 30th of July, 1635, the same correspondent wrote of Lady Purbeck's being "in some part of France, where I wish she may stay, but it seems not good so to the higher powers: for there is of late an express messenger sent to seek her with the Privy Seal of his Majesty to summon her into England, within six weeks after the receipt thereof, which if she do not obey, she is to be proceeded against according to the laws of this Kingdom."

In a letter[92] from the "Rev. Mr. Thomas Garrard to the Lord Deputy," dated 27th April, 1637, there is an announcement which may surprise some readers:—

"Another of my familiar acquaintance has gone over to that Popish religion, Sir Robert Howard, which I am very sorry for. My Lady Purbeck left her country and religion both together, and since he will not leave thinking of her, but live in that detestable sin, let him go to that Church for absolution, for comfort he can find none in ours."

Now, "the Reverend Mr. Garrard" can scarcely have known what Sir Robert would, or would not, "leave thinking of," and, as to his living "in that detestable sin," he and his fellow-sinner had not been even in the same country for nearly two years at the time when Garrard was writing; and, as we have already shown, the unlikelihood of their having committed the sin in question for another couple of years before that may be more than plausibly argued. And it should be remembered that these two people could have no object in becoming Catholics, unless they received the benefits of the Sacraments of the Catholic Church; and as Catholics, they would believe that their confessions would be sacrileges, their absolutions invalid, and their communions the "eating and drinking their own damnation," unless they confessed their immoralities among their other sins, with a firm purpose never to commit them again.

It is clear, therefore, that when they became Catholics Sir Robert Howard and Lady Purbeck must have determined never to resume their illicit intercourse; and, so far as is known, they never did so. In a letter to Secretary Windebanke written from Paris, in July, 1636, Lord Scudamore, after saying something about Lady Purbeck, adds: "She expects every day Sir Robert Howard here:" but this must have been mere gossip, for Scudamore cannot have been in the confidence of that fugitive from England, Lady Purbeck, as he was English Ambassador at Paris; moreover, he was a particular ally of Archbishop Laud,[93] therefore, not likely to have relations with an escaped prisoner of Laud's; although, as we shall presently find, another, although very different, friend of Laud took her part. Nor is there anything to show that Sir

Robert Howard went to Paris.

Respecting the matter of Sir Robert's submission to the Catholic Church, the Reverend Mr. Garrard was perfectly right in saying: "Let him go to that Church for absolution, for comfort he can find none in ours." Whether the Catholic religion is the worst of religions or the best of religions, it is the religion to which those in grievous trouble, whether through misfortune or their own fault, most frequently have recourse; a religion which offers salvation and solace even to the adulterer, the thief, the murderer, or the perpetrator of any other crimes, on condition of contrition and firm purpose of amendment.[94]

FOOTNOTES:

[87] *History of the Troubles and Tryal of Archbishop Laud* (ed. 1695), p. 146.

[88] Vol. I., p. 390, 17th March, 1635.

[89] *Strafford Papers*, Vol. I., p. 447. Letter from Garrard to the Lord Deputy, dated 30th July, 1635.

[90] Lingard, Vol. VII., Chap. V.

[91] *Strafford Letters*, Vol. I., p. 434.

[92] *Ibid.*, Vol. II., p. 72.

[93] "The remarkably studious, pious, and hospitable life he led, made him respected & esteemed by all good men, especially by Laud, who generally visited him in going to & from his Diocese of St. David's & found his entertainment as kind and full of respect as ever he did from any friend" (Burke's *Dormant and Extinct Peerages*, p. 483).

[94] In *Coles' MSS.*, Vol. XXXIII., p. 17, may be found the following note, after a mention of Lady Purbeck: "Sir Robert Howard died April 22, 1653, and was buried at Clunn in Shropshire, leaving issue by Catherine Nevill, his Wife, 3 sons, who, I presume, he married after the Lady Purbeck's death which happened 8 years before his own. The Epitaph in my Book in Folio of Lichfield,

lent me by Mr. Mitton. Sir Robert was 5th Son to Thomas, Earl of Suffolk, Lord Treasurer of England."

CHAPTER XII.

"O must the wretched exile ever mourn,
Nor after length of rolling years return?"

DRYDEN.

LADY PURBECK was not to be left in peace in Paris. As
Garrard had said, a writ was issued commanding her to return
to England upon her allegiance, and it was sent to Paris by a
special messenger who was ordered to serve it upon her, if he
could find her. The matter was placed in the hands of the English
Ambassador, and he describes what followed in a letter[95] from
Paris to the Secretary of State in England:—

"Rt. Honble.

"Your honours letters dated the 7th March—I received the 21
the same style by the Courrier sent to serve his Majesties writt
upon the Lady Viscountesse Purbecke. They came to me about
11 of the clock in the Morning. Upon the instant of his coming
to me I sent a servant of myne own to show him the house, where
the Lady lived publiquely, and in my neighbourhood."

The business in hand, it will be observed, was not to arrest
Lady Purbeck, but simply to serve the writ upon her: a duty which
proved not quite so simple as might be supposed. On arriving
at the house in which Lady Purbeck was living, "the Courrier
taking off his Messengers Badge knocked at the doore to gett
in. There came a Mayd to the doore that would not open it, but
peeped through a grating and asked his businesse. He sayd, he
was not in such hast but he could come againe to-morrow. But

the Mayd and the rest of the household having charge not to open the doore, but to suche as were well knowne, the Messenger could not gett in."

This first failure would not in itself have much alarmed the Ambassador; but he says: "In the afternoone, I understood that the Lady had received notice 15 days before, that a privy seale was to come for her, which had caused her ever since to keep her house close."

This made him nervous, and he tried to push the matter with greater speed.

"We endeavoured by severall ways," he wrote, "to have gotten the Messenger into the house. But having considered and tryed till the next day in the afternoone, we grew very doubtfull that the Messenger might be suspected and that the Lady might slip away from that place of her residence that night."

Unless the writ could be properly served upon her, proceedings against her could not be carried out in England, and, once out of the house in which she now was known, or at least believed, to be, so slippery a lady, as she had already proved herself, would be very difficult to find. To effect an entrance into the house and to serve the writ upon her personally was evidently impossible, and the only alternative was to make sure that she was in the house and then to put the writ into it in such a way that she could not avoid learning of its presence. Therefore, says the Ambassador, "I directed this Bearer to put the Box with the Privy Seale in it through some pane of a lower window into the house and leaving it there to putt on his Badge, and knocking at the doore of the house, if they would not suffer him to enter, then to tell that party, whoe should speak to him at the dore, that he was sent from the K. of Grate Britaine to serve his Majesties Privy Seale upon the Lady Viscountess Purbeck, and that in regard he could not be admitted in, he had left the Privy seale in a Box in such a place of the house, and that in his Majesties name he required the Lady Purbeck to take notice thereof at her perill." So far as getting the Privy Seal inside the house was concerned, all went well. "The Messenger being there, found an upper windowe neath the casements open, and threw up the Box with the Privy seale in it through that windowe into a Chamber, which some say is the Ladies Dining Roome, others, that it is a Chamber of a Man servant waiting upon her."

The writ was now safely lodged in the house; but the Ambassador had ordered the messenger to take care to call the attention of some one in it to the fact that the writ was there. Unfortunately, says the Ambassador, this part of his instructions had been neglected. "The Courrier returnes to me. And finding that he had forgotten to speake at the dore as I had directed him, I caused him presently to returne and to discharge himself in such sort as is above mentioned, which he will depose he did."

This was done, but even then something was still left undone; for it yet remained to be proved that Lady Purbeck was actually in the house at the time when the writ was thrown into it. The Ambassador conceived the idea of obtaining such proof by means of a female witness. For this purpose, he very ingeniously contrived to find a sister of one of Lady Purbeck's servants, and, no doubt by the promise of a heavy bribe, he persuaded her to go to the house, to ask to be admitted in order to speak with her sister, to find out, when there, if Lady Purbeck was in the house, and, if possible, to see her. This ruse was singularly successful, for, as will be seen, the first person whom the girl saw was Lady Purbeck herself.

"A woman being sent to the house under Colour of speaking with a sister of hers the Ladies servant, the Ladye herselfe came downe to the dore, and opening it a little, soe that the woman saw her, she sayd her sister should have leave to go home to her that night. And therefore the Lady was in the house at the same time that the place of her residence was served. She hath lived in that house about a month, and there are (as I am informed) no other dwellers in it but herself."

The writ had now been served, although not into the very hands of Lady Purbeck yet it was hoped sufficiently in order to satisfy the law. But all was not yet smooth. The Ambassador wrote:—

"The morrow after this was done, about midnight, there came some officers with two coaches and 50 archers to divers houses to search for the Lady being directed and instructed by a warrant from the Cardinal that whereas there was a Messenger sent from England to offer some affront to your Lady Purbeck in diminution of this Kings jurisdiction, that therefore they should find out the sayd Lady and protect her."

This intervention on the part of the French Government made Lord Scudamore fear lest *l'affaire Purbeck* might lead to international complications, and he presently adds: "Coming to the knowledge of this particular this Morning I thought good to hasten the Messenger out of the way."

Fortunately for Lady Purbeck, she was not without a friend in Paris. About a year before she went there, a curious character had arrived in the person of Sir Kenelm Digby, a son of the Sir Everard Digby who had been executed for having been concerned in the Gunpowder Plot. Sir Kenelm was well known, both at home and abroad. He had stayed at Madrid with his relative, the Earl of Bristol, at the time when Prince Charles had gone to Spain to woo the Infanta. He had been a brilliant ornament at the Court of Charles I.; but, like all the relations of Bristol, he had been hated by Buckingham. Armed with letters of marque, he had raised a fleet and ravaged the Mediterranean in the character of a privateer. He was literary, philosophical, metaphysical and scientific. When he came to Paris his beautiful wife had been dead a couple of years, and the smart courtier had thrown off his hitherto splendid attire, had clothed himself in black of the very plainest, and had allowed his hair and beard to grow as they would, ragged and untrimmed. Shortly before the arrival of Lady Purbeck in Paris, Sir Kenelm had declared himself a Catholic; and the fact that both he and Lady Purbeck had submitted themselves to the Catholic Church may have formed a bond of union between them. Sir Kenelm soon contrived to interest Cardinal Richelieu in Lady Purbeck's case, and not only Richelieu but also the King and the Queen of France.

A certain "E.R." wrote[96] to Sir R. Puckering: "The last week we had certain news that the Lady Purbeck was declared a papist." And then he went on to say that Louis XIIIth and the Queen of France, as well as Cardinal Richelieu, had sent messages or letters to Charles I., begging him to pardon Lady Purbeck and to allow her to return to England. He also said that the French Ambassador at St. James's was "very zealous in the business." Shortly afterwards he added: "It is said she is altogether advised by Sir Kenelm Digby, who indeed hath written over letters to some of his noble friends of the privy council, wherein he hath set down what a convert this lady is become, so superlatively virtuous and sanctimonious, as the like hath never been seen in men or women; and therefore he does most humbly desire their lordships to farther this lady's peace, and that she may return into England, for otherwise she does resolve to put herself into some monastery. I hear his Majesty does utterly dislike that the lady is so directed by Sir Kenelm Digby, and that she fares nothing better for it."

Of course anybody would naturally sneer at the suggestion that the convert to a religion other than his own could possibly be remarkable for either virtue or sanctity: but there is no visible reason for sympathising with the sneers of (E.R.), or for doubting Sir Kenelm Digby's evidence respecting Lady Purbeck.

It may be a question whether Lady Purbeck ever intended "to put herself into some monastery," in the sense of becoming a nun. She did, however, put herself into a monastery in a very different way. It was, and still is, the custom in some convents to take in lodgers or boarders, either for a short time, for a long time, or even for life. The peace, the quiet, the regularity, and the religious services and observances at such establishments are attractive to some people, especially to those who are in trouble or difficulty. The disadvantages are that, although the lodgers are perfectly free to go where they please and to do what they please, they can generally only get their meals at rigidly appointed hours, that the convent doors are finally closed at a fixed time, usually a very early one; and that after that closing time there is no admittance. Practically the latter arrangement precludes all possibility of society in an evening, and the present writer knows several Catholics of the most unimpeachable orthodoxy, zeal, piety and virtue, who have tried living in convents and monasteries, as boarders, both in Rome and in London, and have given it up simply on account of those inconveniences. It was, therefore, very unjust to speak ill of Lady Purbeck for not having lived in a convent "according to that strictness as was expected," because she left it. But this was done in the following letter:[97] "The Lady Purbeck is come forth of the English Nunnerie. For, the Lady Abbess being from home, somebody forgott to provide the Lady Purbeck her dinner, and to leave the roome open where she used to dine at night, expostulating with the Abbess, they agreed to part fairely, which the Abbess was the more willing unto in regard the Lady Purbeck did not live according to that strictness as was expected. Car. Richelieu helped her into the Nunnerie."

It may be inferred from this letter that Lady Purbeck left the convent for the simple reason that she was not comfortable in it— even the "superlatively virtuous" do not like to be dinnerless— and that, either because she was unpunctual, or because she was inclined to make complaints, the Abbess was relieved when she took her departure. But by Scudamore's own showing they parted "fairely;" or, as we should now say, good friends.

Among Sir Kenelm Digby's English correspondents, while he was in Paris, was Lord Conway, a soldier as devoted to literature as to arms, and a general who always seemed fated to fight under disadvantages. Shortly after the time with which we are at present dealing, he was defeated when in command of the King's troops at Newcastle. Meanwhile, Sir Kenelm was endeavouring to "fit him withal," in the matter of "curious books," from Paris. As the letter[98] from Sir Kenelm to Lord Conway, about to be quoted, has something in it about Lord Wimbledon, it may be well to note that he was a brother of Lady Elizabeth Hatton and therefore an uncle of Lady Purbeck.

After observing that England has been singularly happy in producing men like King Arthur and others who performed actions of only moderate valour or interest, which subsequent ages mistook for great achievements, he says:—

"But none will be more famous and admirable to our Nevewes(?) than the noble valiant and ingenious Peer, the Lord Wimbledone, whose epistle[99] exceedeth all that was ever done before by any so victorious a generall of armies or so provident a governor of townes, I only lament for it that it was not hatched in a season when it might have done the honor to Baronius,[100] his collections, to have bin inserted among them.

"Here is a Lady that he hath reason to detest above all persons in the worlde, if robbing a man of all the portion of witt, courage, generousnesse, and other heroicall partes due to him, do meritt such an inclination of the minde towardes them that have thus bereaved them: for surely the Genius that governeth that family and that distributeth to each of them their shares of natures guiftes was either asleepe, or mistooke (or somewhat else was the cause) when he gave my Lady of Purbecke a dubble proportion of these and all other noble endowments, and left her poore Uncle, so naked and unfurnished: Truly my lord to speake seriously I have not seen more prudence, sweetinesse, goodnesse, honor and bravery shewed by any woman that I know, than this unfortunate lady sheweth she hath a rich stock of. Besides her naturall endowments, doubtlessly her afflictions adde much: or rather have polished, refined and heightened what nature gave her: and you know vexatio dat intellectum. Is it not a shame for you Peeres (and neare about the king) that you will let so brave a lady live as she doth in distress and banishment: when her exile serveth stronger but to conceive scandalously of our nation, that we will not permit those to live among us who have so much worth and goodnesse as this lady giveth show off....

"Yo. Lo: most humble and affectionate

"servant,

"KENELM DIGBY."

Sir Kenelm, like Scudamore, was on a friendly footing with Lady Purbeck's chief enemy, Archbishop Laud, but in a very different sense. When Sir Kenelm was a boy Laud had been his tutor, and a friendship had sprung up between the master and the pupil which was not broken by the conversion of the pupil to a religion greatly disliked by the master. Subsequently, Sir Kenelm gave evidence in favour of his old tutor, before the Committee appointed to prepare the prosecution of Laud at his trial, and he sent kind messages to Laud in the Tower. Unlike Scudamore, however, he was no admirer of Laud's religion or of his ecclesiastical policy, if indeed of any of his policy.

Although Sir Kenelm Digby, the King and the Queen of France, Cardinal Richelieu, and the French Ambassador at the Court of St. James's did their best to obtain forgiveness for Lady Purbeck, Charles I. was long obdurate. At first, as we have seen, he had sent a writ commanding her to return at once to her native country for punishment. When he had withdrawn that writ, he for some time refused to allow her to return at all, for any purpose. But troubles were brewing for Charles himself, and, after Lady Purbeck had spent an exile of some length in Paris, she was permitted to come to England, without any liability to stand barefoot in a white sheet for the amusement of the congregation in a fashionable London church on a Sunday morning.

FOOTNOTES:

[95] *S.P. For.*, Charles I., France. Scudamore to Coke, 25th March—4th April, 1636. This letter was addressed to Sir John Coke, the Secretary of State.

[96] *Court and Times of Charles I.* By D'Israeli, Vol. II., p. 242.

[97] *S.P.*, Charles I., France. Scudamore to Windebank, I/121 July, 1636.

[98] *S.P. Dom.*, Charles I., Vol. CCCXLIV., No. 58. Sir Kenelm Digby to Edward Lord Conway and Kilultagh, 21/31 January, 1637.

[99] Wimbledon was Governor of Portsmouth and the letter in question was probably one mentioned by Walpole in his *Royal and Noble Authors*, to the Mayor of Portsmouth "reprehending him for the Townsmen not pulling off their hats to a Statue of the King Charles, which his Lordship had erected there." Such an "epistle" might well excite the derision and contempt of Sir Kenelm.

[100] The author of *Annales Ecclesiastici.*

CHAPTER XIII.

"To err is human, to forgive divine."

POPE.

CONCERNING Lady Purbeck's life, after her return to England, we have the following evidence from *Coles' Manuscripts*. Let us observe, first, that in the extract there is a mistake. It was not Lady Purbeck, but the wife of her son, whose maiden name was Danvers. Anybody who may choose to discredit the whole, on account of this error, can do so if he pleases; but it is certain that Lord Purbeck "owned the son" and that the son's grandson, "the Rev. Mr. Villiers," claimed "the Title of Earl of Bucks." Therefore we see no reason for doubting the statement that Lord Purbeck "took his Wife again." The "after 16 years" would seem to tally with the undoubted facts.

"[101]Lady Purbeck's name Danvers; absent from Husband 16 years: had by Sir Robert Howard one son who married a Bertie, and took the Title of Lord Purbeck, which Lady Purbeck's will I have. Lord Purbeck after 16 years took his wife again, and owned the Son, which 2nd Lord Purbeck had one Son, Father of the Rev. Mr. Villiers, who now claims the Title of Earl of Bucks. &c."

It will be remembered that even when Lady Purbeck was being proceeded against for unfaithfulness to her husband, at the instigation of Buckingham, she was on friendly terms with Lord Purbeck, and that Buckingham had considerable difficulty in keeping them apart: consequently it is the less to be wondered at that Lord Purbeck "took his wife again," after her return from exile. Not only was Lady Purbeck now a reformed character, but, like Lord Purbeck, she was a convert to the Catholic Church; and this would probably make him the more inclined to receive her again as his wife and to trust her for the future. At the time of their reunion Lady Purbeck must have been about forty, and he must have been an oldish man; although not too old to be a bridegroom, and no longer under suspicion of insanity; for, in addition to starting a second time as husband to Frances, Lady Purbeck, it is recorded that after her death, which occurred in five or six years, he married again,[102] and survived his first wife by twelve years.

If the beginning of married life a second time, after an interval of sixteen years—to say nothing of certain awkward incidents which had transpired in the meantime—may have been a little out of the common, it is more remarkable still that Lord Purbeck should have acknowledged the boy, Robert Wright, as his son. As was shown in an earlier chapter, it is just possible that he may have been ignorant of the fact that the lad was not his own child, or rather, perhaps, that he refused to believe in that fact. On the other hand, as the boy was born in wedlock, he had in any case the right to acknowledge him as such, if he so pleased. That was his concern, not ours, so we need not cavil at it.

His doing so may be accounted for by either of the two following suppositions: namely, that he acknowledged the boy out of affection for, and to please, his wife—possibly it may have been one of the inducements held out to persuade her to return to him—or that he gradually took a fancy to the lad and chose this method of adopting him. Whatever the cause of his acknowledging the boy may have been, that acknowledgment encourages the idea that good relations existed between Lord and Lady Purbeck after what may almost be called their second marriage, or, perhaps still better called, their first real marriage with consent on both sides.

Purbeck called the boy Robert Villiers, and would not allow him to be spoken of as Robert Wright. When the lad came of age, Lord Purbeck made him join with himself, as his son and heir, in the conveyance of some lands, under the name of Robert Villiers,[103] the most formal of legal recognitions.

It is likely that her life soon became that of an invalid, for she died in the year 1645, when staying with her mother at Oxford. In that year the Court of Charles I. was at this town, which may account for her own and her mother's presence there. As we saw, in the first chapter, there is some question as to whether Lady Purbeck was born in the year 1599 or in 1600, so she may have been either forty-five or forty-six at the time of her death. Her life, although of very moderate length, had been one of considerable adventure, which may have told heavily upon her constitution; if her personal concerns were peaceful at the time of her death, we know that the conditions of the King and of the Court, together with the prospects of all of high rank who were loyal to the Crown, were then causing great anxiety and excitement at Oxford: and this may well have had a bad effect upon the health of an invalid.

Of Lady Purbeck's character much less is recorded than of the characters of several other leading figures in this story—her father, her mother, Bacon, Buckingham. We know, however, that she faithfully nursed during his last two years her surly old father, who had treated her abominably and spoiled her life; that she never lost the friendship of Lord Purbeck; that, in her trouble she sought the consolations of religion in a Church which would require a full confession of her sins, accompanied by sincere repentance and virtuous resolutions; that she bore an excellent character in Paris; and that she spent her last years with her husband or her mother. It is true that she had sinned, that she had sinned grievously; but, when we consider her education under parents who were fighting like cat and dog, the marriage which was forced upon her, and the dissolute Court in which she, a singularly beautiful woman, spent the early years of her married life, we may well hesitate before we look for stones to cast at her memory.

And, after all, the only description of her character, of any length, which we have been able to find, namely, that given by Sir Kenelm Digby, is highly favourable. If an apology be required for repeating it, that apology is humbly given.

After declaring that of "wit, courage, generosity, and other heroic parts," nature had given Lady Purbeck "a double share," together with "all other noble endowments," Sir Kenelm says: "I have not seen more prudence, sweetness, honour and bravery shown by any woman that I know, than this unfortunate lady showeth she hath such a rich stock of. Besides her natural endowments, doubtless her afflictions add much; or rather have polished, refined and heightened, what nature gave her."

Even when we have made due allowance for the fact that the pen of Sir Kenelm Digby was inclined to be a little flowery, sufficient is left in this description of Lady Purbeck to make her character attractive, and we know that nature had added to her charms by endowing her with exceptional beauty. No attempt shall be made here to exaggerate either her attractions or her virtues, much less to extenuate or minimise her faults; but let us at least forgive the latter.

There are ladies who call the story of Mary Magdalen "beautiful," yet would on no consideration tolerate a repetition of even its most beautiful incidents, in real life. If she now existed, the greatest concession they would make would be to subscribe towards sending her to a Home for Fallen Women; or, which is more likely, they would ask for an order of admission for her from someone else who subscribed to such an institution. From such we cannot expect a charitable view of *The Curious Case of Lady Purbeck*.

It would be out of place to enter into petty theological questions in a comparatively trivial work such as this—to inquire, for instance, into the question whether it may not be as possible to be damned for detraction as to be damned for adultery; but we may at least believe that Lady Purbeck spent her later years in contrition for the past and virtue in the present.

We have now done with the curious case of Lady Purbeck, and it only remains to say something about the less curious cases of some of her descendants.

It might be supposed that "Robert Wright," who was just of age at the time of his mother's death, would be proud to bear the name of Villiers and to be acknowledged as the rightful heir to the estates and title of Viscount Purbeck. As time went on, however, he became ashamed of those privileges.[104] The son of a Cavalier, he became a Roundhead, and three years after the death of his mother he married one of the daughters and co-heiresses of his relative, Sir John Danvers, subsequently one of the judges who condemned King Charles I. to death.

He eventually obtained a patent from Oliver Cromwell to change his name for that of his wife, declaring that he hated the name of Villiers on account of the mischief which several of those who bore it had done to the Commonwealth; and as to the title of Viscount Purbeck, he disclaimed it with contempt.

But before the Commonwealth Robert Danvers, as he even then called himself, sat in the House of Commons as member for Westbury. When people want titles, they do not always find it easy to obtain them; but, when they do not want them, they cannot always get rid of them. Robert was summoned to the House of Lords, as a peer, to answer the very serious charge of having said that "he hated the Stuarts and that if no person could be found to cut off the King's head, he would do it himself." He refused to attend, on the ground that he was not a member of the House of Lords but of the House of Commons. This plea was not allowed, and he was actually compelled to kneel at the bar of the House of Lords and to beg pardon for his criminal words.

At the Restoration he remained an obstinate Roundhead, and, instead of showing any desire to claim the title of Viscount Purbeck, he obtained permission from Charles II. to levy a fine of his titles in possession and in remainder. Then he retired to an estate which he owned in the parish of Houghton in Radnorshire, bearing the curious name of Siluria. He died in the year 1676, at

Calais, and in his will he is described as "Robert Danvers, alias Villiers, Esq."

Robert's wife survived him, and, now that he and his idiosyncrasies were safely out of the way, it occurred to this daughter of a regicide that "the Right Honourable the Dowager Viscountess Purbeck" would sound much more euphonious than "the widow Danvers;" accordingly—solely for the sake of others—she adopted that title. At the same time, her two sons, Robert and Edward, resumed the name of Villiers.

Immediately after the death of his father, Robert, the elder of the two sons, took as much trouble to get summoned to the House of Lords as his father had taken to escape from it. He sent a petition on the subject to Charles II., who referred him to the House of Lords. His claim was opposed. First, on the ground that his father had barred his right to honours by the fine which he had levied, *i.e.*, by renouncing those honours, and, secondly, on the ground that his father had not been a son of John Villiers, First Viscount Purbeck, but a son of Sir Robert Howard. A petition[105] against the claim was presented by the Earl of Denbigh, who professed himself "highly concerned in the honour of the Duke of Buckingham and his sister, the Duchess of Richmond & Lennox; Petitioner's mother, Susanna, having been the only sister of the late Duke of Buckingham," and he prayed "the House to examine the truth of these assertions, before allowing itself to be contaminated by illegitimate blood."

This warning to the Lords against contaminating itself by illegitimate blood, at a time when Charles II. was constantly enriching it with his own illegitimate offspring, or what at least purported to be so, is rather entertaining. On the other hand, in support of the claim, the claimant's counsel professed to be able to prove the legitimacy of Robert Villiers, alias Wright.[106]

The House of Lords after considering the matter petitioned the King to allow the introduction of a Bill to disable Robert from claiming the title of Viscount Purbeck: but seven peers opposed this petition stating in writing that "the said claimant's right ...

did, both at the hearing at the bar and debate in the House, appear to them clear in fact and law and above all objection." Charles II. replied that he "would take it into consideration." This appears to have been the last official word ever pronounced upon the subject, and nobody has since then been summoned to the House of Lords as Viscount Purbeck.

The claimant, however, continued to call himself Lord Purbeck. He came to an early end, being killed in a duel by Colonel Luttrell, at Liège, when he was only twenty-eight; but he left a son. Nor did this son only call himself Lord Purbeck, for on the death of the childless second Duke of Buckingham, of whom Dryden wrote:—[107]

Stiff in opinion—always in the wrong—
Was everything by starts, but nothing long;
Who in the course of one revolving moon
Was chemist, fiddler, statesman and buffoon.
Then all for women, painting, rhyming, drinking:
Besides a thousand freaks that died in thinking;

John Villiers, alias Danvers, alias Wright, in addition to the title of Viscount Purbeck, assumed that of Earl of Buckingham, the reversion of which had been secured by the first Earl and Duke to his brother and his heirs, in the case of his own direct heirs failing. This self-styled Earl squandered his fortune in a life of debauchery, and then married the daughter of a clergyman, a widow with a large jointure but about as dissolute in character as himself, which is saying much. He left no sons.

Such claims as there were to the titles of Purbeck and Buckingham then lay with the Rev. George Villiers, Rector of Chalgrove, in Oxfordshire. He was the son of Edward, the second son of the boy christened Robert Wright. In the year 1723, on the death of his cousin, the so-called Earl of Buckingham, this clergyman put in a claim to the titles of Earl of Buckingham and Viscount Purbeck; but, unlike his cousin, he does not appear to have ever "lorded" himself.

This cleric left a son named George, who also became a parson, and Vicar of Frodsham in Cheshire. Efforts were made in his youth to obtain for him a summons to the House of Lords; but, in addition to the doubtful character of his claims, he was no *persona grata* to the King, as he was known to be an ardent Jacobite. As Burke says: "Republicans during the reign of the Stuarts—Jacobites during the reign of the Guelphs—this unfortunate family seems always to have had hold of the wrong end of the stick." As a rule, they appear to have held that end of it, but certainly it is a rule to which George Villiers, first Duke of Buckingham, was a remarkable exception.

The Rev. George Villiers, who still owned property which had been settled by Sir Edward Coke on his daughter, Lady Purbeck, died without issue, in 1774, and his brother died a bachelor. The male line of Villiers, alias Danvers, alias Wright, then expired. We hear no more of any claims to the Purbeck peerage; henceforward the title which stands at the head of this story was no longer to have any place in living interests. At this point, let us also take leave of it; and the author hopes that his readers, if ever reminded of this book by the mention of Lady Purbeck, may not exclaim in the words of a character in Macbeth:—"The devil himself could not pronounce a title more hateful to mine ear."

FOOTNOTES:

[101] *Coles' MSS.*, Vol. XXXIII., p. 17.
[102] He married a daughter of Sir William Slingsby of Kippax, Yorkshire.
[103] Burke's *Extinct and Dormant Peerages*.
[104] The authorities for most of what follows are *The Historical MSS. Commission*, Ninth Report, Part II., p. 58; *MSS. of the House of Lords*, 30th April, 5th May, and 3rd June, 1675, 14th March, 16th June, and 9th July, 1678, and Burke's *Extinct and Dormant*

Peerages.

[105] *MSS. of the House of Lords*, 228, 30th April, 1675.

[106] *MSS. of the House of Lords*, 228, 30th April, 1675.

[107] *Absalom and Achitophel*, line 447, *seq.*

www.ingramcontent.com/pod-product-compliance
Lightning Source LLC
Chambersburg PA
CBHW030845090426
42737CB00009B/1112